"*Being Better* is a gentle and clear introduction to living a Stoic life. It is like no other introductory book on Stoicism: it does not promise you the moon, it does not preach, and it does not even tempt you with the 'best' life — only a better one. If you want to live like a Stoic in the modern world without having to 'update' Stoicism, *Being Better* is for you. In this short book, the authors bring to life ancient Stoic principles with modern examples. Their examples include many non-Stoic practitioners of Stoic principles, such as Pat Tillman, Rosa Parks, Alex Zanardi, and Nick Hanauer. It is surprising that the authors could cover so much ground in so few pages and yet be so clear. I think it is one of the best introductions to modern Stoicism." **— Dr. Chuck Chakrapani**, editor of *The Stoic* magazine, Distinguished Visiting Professor at Ryerson University, and author of *Unshakable Freedom*

"Do you want to live a life worth living? Try Stoicism. Do you want to try Stoicism? Read *Being Better* and let it be your guide." **— Massimo Pigliucci**, author of *A Field Guide to a Happy Life*

"Kai and Leonidas vividly present the power and promise of the Stoic way of life and its profound relevance to the issues we face today. They gather a chorus of timeless insights and questions — from Zeno, Cleanthes, Musonius, and others — that challenge us to discover well-being, not only for ourselves but for those around us, too. Highly recommended!" **— Stephen Hanselman**, *New York Times* bestselling coauthor of *Lives of the Stoics*, *The Daily Stoic*, and *The Daily Stoic Journal*

"The timeless lessons of Stoicism are more relevant than ever. In a time of disorder, *Being Better* is just what we need to bring them to light." **— Chris Guillebeau**, author of *The Money Tree* and *The $100 Startup*

"*Being Better* shows why Stoicism is the go-to philosophy for our time. Kai Whiting and Leo Konstantakos give a splendid account of the ancient Stoic teachers and their relevance to such issues as communal living and sustainability. Their book stands out for its sincerity and its exploration of what it means to cultivate Stoic virtues here and now." **— Anthony Long**, Professor Emeritus of Classics and Literature at the University of California, Berkeley, and author of *Epictetus: How to Be Free — An Ancient Guide to the Stoic Life*

BEING BETTER

BEING BETTER

STOICISM FOR A WORLD WORTH LIVING IN

KAI WHITING and LEONIDAS KONSTANTAKOS

New World Library
Novato, California

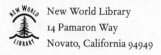 New World Library
14 Pamaron Way
Novato, California 94949

Text design by Megan Colman

Library of Congress Cataloging-in-Publication Data

Names: Whiting, Kai, author. | Konstantakos, Leonidas, author.
Title: Being better : stoicism for a world worth living in / Kai Whiting and Leonidas Konstantakos.
Description: Novato, California : New World Library, [2021] | Includes bibliographical references and index. | Summary: "Explains the ethical principles of the ancient Greek philosophy known as Stoicism and shows how it can change our understanding of contemporary issues such as environmental sustainability, social justice, and global capitalism"-- Provided by publisher.
Identifiers: LCCN 2020054852 (print) | LCCN 2020054853 (ebook) | ISBN 9781608686933 (paperback) | ISBN 9781608686940 (epub)
Subjects: LCSH: Stoics. | Conduct of life.
Classification: LCC B528 .W49 2021 (print) | LCC B528 (ebook) | DDC 188--dc23
LC record available at https://lccn.loc.gov/2020054852
LC ebook record available at https://lccn.loc.gov/2020054853

First printing, April 2021
ISBN 978-1-60868-693-3
Ebook ISBN 978-1-60868-694-0
Printed in Canada on 100% postconsumer-waste recycled paper

 New World Library is proud to be a Gold Certified Environmentally Responsible Publisher. Publisher certification awarded by Green Press Initiative.

10 9 8 7 6 5 4 3 2 1

To all the Stoics who trod the path before me, to those who walk alongside me, and to those of you who will follow in my footsteps.
— Kai

To Marian Demos, who saw the life of a Stoic as nearly unattainable — and then faced illness, pain, and death like one.
— Leo

CONTENTS

CHAPTER 1

THE PROMISE
OF THE "GOOD LIFE"

Well-being is realized by small steps, but is truly no small thing.
— Zeno of Citium, as quoted by Diogenes Laertius,
Lives of the Eminent Philosophers 7.1.26[1]

More than two thousand years ago, a penniless immigrant, Zeno of Citium, argued that there is only one destination worthy of a lifetime journey. That destination is *eudaimonia*.* This Greek term refers to a state of being that we tend to translate into English as "happiness," "flourishing," "fulfillment," "well-being," or the "good life." Zeno believed that the path toward *eudaimonia* is open to all and that reaching it is the ultimate purpose and highest aim for humankind, regardless of gender, ethnicity, education level, social status, or general life experience.† He shared

---

* For Zeno, *eudaimonia* represents a destination, rather than a journey, because you either reach it or you don't, in the same way either you are in Miami or you're not (if you are near Miami or almost in Miami, you are still not there).

† Our interpretation of the Stoic texts is that the only time this does not apply is when a severe mental disability or cognitive condition, which cannot be rectified with medical treatment or psychological intervention, acts as an insurmountable barrier to someone's ability to enjoy the fullness of the prototypical human experience.

1

his ideas regarding *eudaimonia* at the *Stoa Poikile* — the "Painted Porch" — a colonnade that stood outside the public market in Athens. Although its ruins might not look like much today, Zeno's followers, the Stoics, took the colonnade's name, not Zeno's, to describe their very public approach to philosophy. Then as now, Stoic ideas didn't take long to spread and take root in people's hearts and minds.

In many ways, this book is a contemporary version of Zeno's presence at the Painted Porch. We wrote it for all those who, as they walk through the proverbial public square, believe that they could live the "good life" and are willing to put in the work to achieve it. Stoicism is a practical philosophy that provides an antidote for troubled times, while it also keeps our ego and excesses in check when things are going well. Stoicism helps us to understand ourselves and other people better and to navigate a path through life's challenges and successes. Zeno and his Stoics understood that the "good life" is rooted in communal living, which includes partaking in civic duties, building strong local ties, and being open to, and appreciative of, the universal community that extends across the whole world.

Stoicism won't remove all of life's obstacles, but it helps us to think differently about them. It won't provide us with all the answers, but it gives us the ability to form the questions that ultimately lead to the solutions. Stoicism may be more than two thousand years old, but Zeno's wisdom is as powerful as ever.

In the ancient world, Stoicism was practiced by a wide variety of people, some of whom you will meet in the coming chapters, as we consider how Stoicism can improve our lives today. These include Zeno himself, who was a merchant; his student, Cleanthes, who was an ex-boxer and a laborer by night; and another two students, Chrysippus, who was a former long-distance runner, and Sphaerus, an educator. Sphaerus took Stoicism to Sparta and worked alongside a Spartan king and queen to reform the city's laws and warrior schools (*agoge*). A century later, Panaetius, a member of a prestigious and celebrated family, reenvisioned Stoic ideas and used his political and social capital to promote Stoic learning among the Roman elite, which led to Stoicism becoming the philosophy of choice for statesmen of the Senate. These included Cato the Younger, who, in line with Stoic principles, took a stand against the tyranny of Julius Caesar. Stoicism also inspired the first-century philosophy teacher Musonius Rufus, who withstood exile (twice!) and once stood in the way of an imminent battle in an attempt to prevent it. Emperor Marcus Aurelius leaned on Stoic philosophy during his many war campaigns against the Germanic tribes. Stoicism drove scientific inquiry and encouraged the polymath Posidonius to travel far and wide in his quest for knowledge. Stoicism also gave hope to those situated on the lowest rungs of the social ladder, none more famously than the disabled slave Epictetus, whose lectures, written in the common vernacular, would thousands of years later be appreciated by all those looking for the promise of the "good life."

Why has Stoicism endured, and why is it useful for us today? Because, in short, it provides us with useful tools and methods for reflecting upon, and reframing, our thoughts so that they serve rather than impede us, so that they build rather than destroy our communities, however difficult a challenge we face. In the modern world, Stoicism is known to have helped prisoners of war, including Vice Admiral James Stockdale, and those sent to concentration camps, such as Dr. Viktor Frankl, to find meaning and persevere in the face of torture.[2] It has inspired those of high political office, including Theodore Roosevelt, to carefully consider and deliver on their decisions.[3] More recently, Stoicism was used by the software engineer and American writer Susan Fowler to survive, and then blow the whistle on, her tech employer's highly toxic work culture. In fact, Fowler's Stoic-influenced sense of courage and justice led her to write the 2017 blog piece that kick-started Silicon Valley's own #MeToo moment.[4]

Stoicism is equally valuable for those facing long-term unemployment or those unfortunate enough to contract an incurable disease.* It can help parents who are looking for advice on child raising or those who have just lost their parents and are tasked with clearing out their belongings. It can help you decide how best to spend and save your money, whether you have a little or a lot. It can assist you in selecting a career or retirement plan.

Both Leo and I,† this book's authors, have discovered the healing, practical benefits of Stoic philosophy in our own lives. For me personally, no moment has been more profound than the afternoon in January 2016 when my grandmother, Sheila, died. A week previously, she had been taken ill with a heart condition, surprising everyone, given her active lifestyle. As Sheila was the rock upon which my family was built, I was convinced she would pull through. It wasn't that I had never considered the possibility of her death, rather that such an abstract thought had always slipped away before I could dwell on it. Therefore, it wasn't until her passing was announced in the hospital waiting room that I realized the gravity of the situation. Memories of her would remain, but no new ones could be created. In that moment, it dawned on me that I would go on to do and say many things, but Sheila

---

* The late modern Stoic philosopher Lawrence Becker contracted polio as a small child, a disease that left him with upper body paralysis. Stoicism informed his professional and personal life so much so that he went on to play a key role in disseminating Stoic ideas to new audiences.

† While this book is cowritten, and each author is an equal contributor, we decided that Kai would speak in the first person and Leo would not; this is to enhance readability. Thus, we use "Leo and I" when we want to refer to or distinguish ourselves as individuals.

would no longer see or hear them. For the first time, I understood the finality of death. The immediate feelings were pain and sadness, but it was the inability to change things, the impossibility of sharing new life milestones and successes with her, that cut the deepest and lingers on.

Sheila's death triggered an urgent need for me to reprioritize my life purpose, which up until that point had been focused on becoming a prestigious university professor rather than a better *person*. While there is nothing wrong with wanting to succeed professionally in life, it is not more important than developing a good relationship with oneself and others. I didn't feel regret, for such an emotion felt pointless, especially as I couldn't turn back the clock or bring back the dead. However, I wanted to construct a future where I would have the presence of mind to pay more attention to the things and people I cared about. I didn't want to lose someone else before I adjusted my values. I decided to make this change the moment I left the hospital and every day after that. The next question I faced was *how* to become better.

Call it luck, fate, or destiny, I didn't have to look far for answers. They were already in my hands, contained in a book that I had brought along to make the anxious hospital visits a little more bearable. The book focused on the wisdom of the Roman emperor Marcus Aurelius, the most famous Stoic philosopher. The more I read, the more I became convinced that the path to being a better person started and ended with Stoicism.

The power of Stoicism lies in its unique view on what it means to be happy, that is, to achieve *eudaimonia*. This state does not depend on eliminating life's perils and potholes. Stoicism works because it is designed to help us find meaning and take positive action regardless of our circumstances and how we feel about them. It asks us to commit to seeking and progressing in virtue rather than mere pleasure, to value long-term character building over short-term gains, and to hold ourselves accountable to our own moral code rather than adhering to arbitrary rules or following practices promoted by the latest celebrity or guru. Stoicism isn't focused on esoteric or abstract matters. It is not about specific practices or philosophical life hacks or strategies for getting ahead. Nor does it offer up tips or tricks for shaping our abs, gaining likes on social media, doubling our salary overnight, or tidying up our living space. Instead, it makes it very clear that becoming the best version of ourselves involves striving for an excellent character — one that can effectively help us create a world worth living in — both for ourselves and for others.

ᚱᚱᚱᚱ

Stoic philosophy has its origins in what most would consider a catastrophic business failure. Zeno,* then a merchant, aged thirty, was on his way to Athens aboard a ship carrying his precious cargo of a purple dye called "royal purple." This dye was so expensive that only the elite could afford to wear clothes of that color,† and thus its sale was going to make Zeno a rich man. However, as fortune would have it, the ship went down in a storm, and just like that, Zeno's business prospects drained into the sea. Zeno survived, but as he sat soaked on the shore at Athens, his gratefulness over being alive soon warped into nervousness. With

---

* There is very little surviving evidence of Zeno's life. With the little we have, Leo and I have tried to piece together his life's "flow," and with some evidence-based speculation on our part, we present in this book an insider's view on Zeno's journey into Stoicism.

† Extracted from the blood of the rare Murex sea snail, this dye was, interestingly enough, the one that the Stoic emperor Marcus Aurelius mentions when he reminds himself in *Meditations* that even the royal color of purple is, in the end, only the blood of dead shellfish. "Royal purple" thus connects the first and last of the famous ancient Stoics.

nothing to sell, Zeno was no longer a merchant as much as a destitute immigrant far away from his home in Cyprus. Just a few hours ago, he had been picturing an altogether different kind of life, dreams now dashed like the wrecked hull he could see bobbing up and down on the waves. How would he ever rebuild his business? How would he repay his suppliers' loans? What did fate have in store for him? Ultimately, *what did this all mean?*

Sitting alone, Zeno could not answer these difficult questions, so he set off on a two-hundred-mile round trip to seek guidance from the Oracle of Delphi — the priestess of the Greek god Apollo — who was respected and revered all over Greece for her divinations. Even kings would travel for days to seek her counsel, and while today it might seem ridiculous to heed the utterings of a young woman in a trancelike state, a trip to Delphi was taken very seriously indeed. Every meeting was an involved process that had more in common with South American ayahuasca rituals than, say, visiting a clairvoyant. The Oracle required visitors to prepare in both body and mind, and as with ayahuasca ceremonies, those seeking answers at the Temple at Delphi had to adhere to strict rules in order to approach the ritual with reverence, respect, and sincerity. You couldn't just rock up to the Oracle, hand over some coins, and demand that she saw you. Nobody could sit in the Oracle's presence until they had properly considered the dangers of misinterpreting her advice and also understood and pledged to abide by the three maxims of self-discovery: "know yourself," "nothing to excess," and "surety brings ruin."[5] Wisdom seekers were told to listen carefully to what she said in relation to their strengths, weaknesses, personal quirks, and the specific roles they played in the wider world (as, say, a daughter, mother, Spartan queen).

Zeno kept all this in mind as he told the Oracle the story of his shipwreck, and she advised him to "take on the pallor of the dead." On his return journey home, Zeno weighed her cryptic words carefully because it was imperative that he interpret them well. What could they possibly mean? As Zeno approached Athens' city gate, it occurred to him that, above all, he must commit to pursuing the ancient wisdom that had been passed down by venerated, and now long-dead, philosophers. He promised himself that he would reexamine the kinds of philosophical texts his own father had read to him while still a boy. In particular, he was determined to get hold of the ones that spoke about the "good life"; that is to say, a life *worth living*, not just one that is (or will ever be) easy, comfortable, or pleasant.

In line with the Oracle's prophecy, at the precise moment when Zeno was reading about Socrates, who Greek philosophers considered the wisest man to have ever lived, another well-known philosopher, Crates of Thebes, happened to stroll by. The two struck up a conversation, Crates agreed to mentor Zeno, and so began Zeno's journey toward *eudaimonia*. In time, Zeno would declare that the "good life" is open to all who actively search for it because, he argued, while wealth is typically preferred to poverty and full health typically preferred to illness, neither is essential to happiness. For evidence, he pointed to all the people who were both wealthy and healthy and yet still lived a life of misery. The universality of flourishing, based on the belief that *eudaimonia* is available to all, was not a position everyone agreed with. The Athenian elite, including Aristotle and his followers, believed that the "good life" could only be attained by those who had certain qualifications: the "right" education, male gender, good looks, and Athenian citizenship. For Zeno, they couldn't have been more wrong.

In order to reach all those in Athens who were interested in pursuing the "good life," Zeno took up a position on the Painted Porch, which was the entryway into the city's central market, the most important shopping mall of its day. Why did he choose this particular location? For one thing, it was the perfect place to master the art of dialogue and negotiation because it was frequented by just about everyone — Athenians and immigrants, slaves and slaveholders, the wealthiest members of society and the poorest living in the streets. For another, the porch's design allowed Zeno to engage with those who might otherwise have walked by. On hearing his message, many in the crowd understood that their lives and their hometowns could become so much more, as long as they set their sights on *eudaimonia* rather than mere existence.

Zeno's particularly austere and disciplined approach to Stoicism was not to claim bragging rights or to refocus his business priorities after his dye had been washed into the sea.* In fact, he often remarked that he had "made a prosperous voyage" only after his cargo had sunk, precisely because his commercial ruin made him care more deeply about the things that mattered. Not wealth or status but the development of an excellent character and a cosmopolitan spirit, values exemplified by a commitment to making the world a better place for yourself and others.

Zeno's good character eventually earned him widespread fame and respect. Before long, he had won the Athenians over to Stoicism. Of course, had he been only self-serving, virtue-signaling, or playing poverty from the comfort of a huge estate, the Athenians would not have cared who he was or what he said. But care they did, and in sufficient numbers to give him the keys to the city and offer him Athenian citizenship — an honor that he politely refused. Posthumously, a statue was erected of him in recognition of the positive impact he had made on the world through

---

* The Greek comedian Philemon could not help but highlight (in his work *Philosophers*) Zeno's uncanny ability to teach hunger and yet still get lots of pupils!

the establishment and leadership of the Stoa (Stoicism's philosophical school) and the path he had cleared for others to venture down. This path isn't easy to follow. This is because Zeno made it clear that a person's ability to progress toward the "good life" rests on the enactment of principles and not simply on blindly following rules.

A principle is a proposition or value that guides our thoughts, actions, and judgment. It is the essence of our moral operating system, and not unlike a compass, it directs our steps. Given that the signposts on the Stoic path are principles rather than rules and regulations, we must think for ourselves every step of the way. No quote on a fridge or scribble in a journal will change that fact. Nothing provides insight if we don't take the time to check our bearings and ready ourselves for the twists and turns that lie ahead.

The need to distinguish between rules and principles is something that Epictetus, an ancient Roman Stoic philosopher, warned us about 350 years after Zeno's death (*Discourses* 1.1): "If you're writing to a friend, grammar will tell you what letters you ought to choose, but as to whether or not you ought to write to your friend, grammar won't tell you that."[6]

In effect, what Epictetus is saying is that no one can tell you how to live your life because *you* must reason for yourself and live accordingly — you must take Stoic principles and make them work for you. You must choose which rules or practices can be accepted and integrated or rejected and dismissed. Sooner or later, you must also decide if you stand for something or if you are just standing around, letting others speak up, waiting for them to make the difference in the world, your world.

Zeno held that excellent character must be the guiding light for our interactions with other people and the world around us, exemplified by our adherence and enactment of the four Stoic virtues of courage, justice, self-control, and wisdom. For instance, if you decide to change your diet to avoid coffee and become a vegetarian — perhaps to be healthier and save money — remember that this also affords you with a wonderful opportunity to express all the Stoic virtues, not just self-control. Making wiser choices about what to eat could include learning about commercial food production and fair trade and changing where you shop and who you buy food from. As you save money and consider the Stoic virtue of justice, you might spend some of the savings on just causes by supporting local or grassroot initiatives. You could invest money in a small start-up that aims to bring local produce to people's doors or join neighbors who are developing a communal garden. Such actions are in line with the ancient Stoic practice of bringing people into our inner circle, or under our wing. They also help us better understand what needs to be done and what lies within our power to make the world a nicer place.

Self-restraint, merely for the sake of it, does not support the common good and thus falls way short of the Stoic ideal. In fact, the ancient Greeks, in general, weren't shy about calling out those people who failed to support the common good because they spent too much time on themselves or their business affairs. They certainly didn't regard them as geniuses. Nor did they wish to emulate them. In fact, they referred to them as *idiōtēs*, quite literally, "idiots." This is why Zeno and his students (particularly Sphaerus, whom we will get to know in chapter 7) admired Spartan discipline. Spartan warriors were praised if they continued to fight after having lost a helmet, as it offered them only personal protection, but they were admonished if they discarded their shield, since this endangered their fellow soldiers, whose survival depended on tight interlocking shield formations.

This nuanced understanding of the Spartan code of conduct is a far cry from the egotistical and macho Sparta of pop culture or indeed from the type of Stoic philosophy that gets promoted by "experts" on social media, life-hacking blogs, and in mainstream newspapers.[7] While not all bad, many articles that promote Stoicism today are written by people who mistake business acumen for virtue.[8]

Stoicism is a big tent that caters to all walks of life, but people who are only interested in themselves and refuse to engage in anything that might perturb their peace are not pursuing Stoicism. They are pursuing Epicureanism. The Greek philosophical school of Epicureanism developed out of a garden owned by Epicurus (341–270 BCE). He held that the goal of human life was "happiness" and that it was achieved by the absence of physical pain and mental disturbance. Various ancient Stoics wrote at length about why they disagreed with him. Stoicism has always been a self-help philosophy with a twist, precisely because it helps us to develop the critical thinking skills and moral accountability that stop us from mistaking *feeling* better with *being* better. As Zeno taught, being better means that we are more intentional in our progress toward living virtuously.

Stoicism isn't *only* about contemplating and working toward our own sense of happiness. How could it be? Zeno describes the road to *eudaimonia* as one paved with conscious and consistent acts of thinking and acting wisely, bravely, justly, and temperately. Nothing in Stoicism is merely done for our own sake. In fact, a Stoic would go as far as to say that if our thoughts, actions, and attitude do not benefit the whole (world, country, community, family, and so on), then we are very much mistaken in thinking that they will benefit us!

For Leo and me, the impact of Stoicism on our daily lives is perhaps most noticeable in our attitudes and actions concerning the ethics of our consumer choices. Our academic research and our desire to live a Stoic lifestyle (not just talk or write about it) have led us to think deeply about the interconnection of all things, especially when it comes to how our actions can cause others to pollute the air, soil, and water on our behalf. Also, as both of us want to be good people, by which we mean not cruel or carelessly contributing to cruelty, we are becoming increasingly careful about which animal products we buy and from whom. Since we first started journeying on the Stoic path together, we have both revisited many of our habits and opinions. For example, given our ages and personal circumstances, we have reconsidered our consumption of dairy in line with our desire to strive for the four Stoic virtues of courage, justice, self-control, and wisdom. Leo and I live in major cities in countries — the United States and Portugal, respectively — that are progressively more aware of plant-based diets, which means we have access to nondairy alternatives that people in other places do not. If we were living in more remote communities, where obtaining vegetal milks or refusing dairy would not be viable nor reasonable, we would have to amend our decision. The same is true when it comes to health concerns. Since we are not currently subject to health conditions that require us to drink cow's milk, our consumption is optional. Here is how we have approached this choice through the four Stoic virtues:

- **Courage:** We recognize that it takes guts (and good organization) to confront governments and corporations over how dairy products are sourced and the ways in which sentient beings are treated. We also understand that courage often starts with saying no, which can prompt lots of unsolicited criticism over food choices. In one sense, "courageously" deciding not to drink milk is relatively trivial compared to other things, but it is not so trivial for the cow who is forcibly separated from her calf and confined to a few square meters of misery. It is also far

from trivial for those people at risk of becoming environmental refugees because intensive agricultural practices
not only harm animals but can cause irrevocable damage
to the environment.

- **Justice:** We take the time to research and deeply consider
how, and to what extent, industrialized dairy production
is linked to forced migration and ecosystem deterioration
triggered by climate breakdown. We are also very careful to evaluate, based on facts and not mere emotion, the
ways in which intensive farming practices cause harm to
the animals and people working in the agricultural and
food sectors. We are particularly concerned with the
power conglomerates have over family-run businesses,
many of which are bankrupted for taking a more compas-
sionate approach to animal husbandry and environmental stewardship.

- **Self-control:** Leo and I like the taste of milkshakes and
dairy ice cream, so maintaining a dairy-free life takes a
certain amount of discipline or self-control, especially
when we would prefer to go to family dinners without
making a fuss. Certain vegan choices make our grocery
bill more expensive, too, and while it doesn't bankrupt us,
the cost adds up. Then again, a principle is not a principle
until it costs you. We feel it is irresponsible to favor our
taste buds over the well-being of the planet and the animals that provide us with milk.

- **Wisdom:** Leo and I try to learn all we can about what we
eat, since we make decisions about food every day. We
strive to make the right decisions by following principles
instead of ignorantly eating polluting, unhealthy, and un-
ethically, if not cruelly, produced food — just because it
is the cheapest and easiest to buy. Of course, as we try to

make the right decision, we need to reassess our choices as and when more comprehensive information comes to light. The important thing to remember is that in Stoicism wisdom isn't about being all-knowing or always right. Wise people make decisions based on the information they have at the time, but they know they might not have all the information they need. They also know circumstances change, and that not everything turns out as expected. This means that a wise person might take an action that seems prudent, given the evidence available, when in actual fact it is not. However, the factual mistake wouldn't mean that the decision taken wasn't reasonable, that it was morally wrong, or that the person taking it lacked good judgment. For example, a wise person might choose to recycle all their plastic packaging in order to avoid harm to the environment. However, a lot of recycled material in the United States, for example, is either landfilled or dumped illegally. Yet the wise person is hardly at fault if they have no reasonable way of knowing whether this is the "recycling" standard of their local waste collector. That said, upon learning new facts, we are all morally obliged to change our behavior, though the best thing to do will depend on who we are and our circumstances. In Stoicism, there is no single right answer or universal solution beyond a commitment to continually reevaluating and learning how to live out the four virtues. In this respect, the wise person's job is never done.

Leo and I don't restrict our food choices because we derive pleasure in being picky, awkward, or sanctimonious. We don't do it because we want to tick a box or be well-regarded within a certain vegetarian or vegan community. We don't do it to impress the neighbors or to prove to ourselves how disciplined we are. Choosing not to do something requires discipline, but if building discipline were the goal, we'd join (or rejoin) the army. Avoiding dairy is one small way we try to live out Stoic values and principles by fostering a better world. The Roman senator Seneca wrote in a letter advising on living a Stoic lifestyle (*Letters to Lucilius* 95.57), "An action will not be right unless one's intention is right."[9] Of course, we are far from perfect and do succumb to lapses or errors in judgment. However, we don't dwell on our mistakes or beat ourselves up about them because that is not what Stoicism calls for. Instead, it asks us to humbly recognize that the most important thing is that we are on the right path, looking the right way, and (hopefully) edging toward *eudaimonia*.

Another aspect to Stoicism is that it helps avoid extremism, which is its own form of ignorance. While Leo and I do not buy or drink dairy products at home, when we are elsewhere, particularly when we are guests in someone else's home, we sometimes make adjustments. Both of our extended families drink cow's milk, and we respect the fact that for their own reasons they continue to do so. Stoically, we are called to take care of and consider others, which is why we do not *always* refuse a kindly offered white coffee or tea. After all, there is virtue in how we treat those who offer hospitality. In other words, even though Leo and I choose not to drink cow's milk in an *ideal* situation, because of the unjust way it is produced commercially, there is also no Stoic argument to support the idea that drinking dairy milk is *always* bad. Deciding to be gracious, polite guests is one situation that calls for flexibility, especially when refusing milk might seem rude or could embarrass our hosts.

From a Stoic perspective, deciding the best action will always *depend* on our *present* circumstances. The key to unlocking our position can be found in the kinds of questions we ask ourselves. In this example of whether to drink milk, we might ask any combination of the following questions: "Where am I?" "Who am I with?" "What's my relationship like with that person?" "Is this an appropriate time and place to explain my reasons for not drinking milk?" "How is the person making the offer likely to react to my refusal?" "Would it be seen as rude to ask if they have a nondairy alternative?" "How many times have I refused tea or coffee today and am I willing to do so again?" and even "Do I want to drink milk?" As these questions show, when deciding upon an appropriate course of action, context is key. Whatever we decide, in any situation, is secondary to the process of rationally arriving at the answer according to the facts at hand.[10]

The flexibility of the Stoic approach means that there are no sets of prescribed answers. To emphasize this, each chapter in this book ends with one or two questions based on the Stoics we've discussed and the issues they've raised. It is only in deep questioning that Stoicism works. Leo and I aren't interested in providing a step-by-step program for improvement. We aren't privy to your personal circumstances. We don't know the nature of the problems you are trying to solve. We cannot guess how you and those around you would react to any of the many possible options available to you. Even if we did know you well and tried to "put ourselves in your shoes," what we would actually be doing is considering your situation from our point of view. In other words, we would be putting our feet into your shoes rather than considering how your shoes fit your feet!

The terrain you will cover, should you choose to pursue the Stoic lifestyle, is far from easy, but it is certainly worth doing! The first step in such a journey is deciding and actively demonstrating that you are ready to set off in the direction of what Zeno called the "good life" or the "life worth living." If you are ready to take that step, then we invite you to come and join us for the rest of the way!

ZENO'S QUESTIONS

When Zeno was shipwrecked, he lost all his cargo. It was certainly an expensive dye, but in losing it he gained something far more valuable: the map to *eudaimonia*.

- A tornado is coming and could destroy your home and all that is in it. Taking only what you could carry or place in a midsize rucksack within five minutes, what do you exit your home with? What does the list of things say about you and what you deem important?

When the ancient Greeks and their neighbors visited the Oracle of Delphi, they passed through a door that had the inscription "Know yourself." This reminded those seeking guidance that the key to interpreting her advice was in understanding who they were.

- When was the last time you asked yourself, "Who am I?" What was your response? How did you come to those conclusions? What character flaws did you ignore or downplay? What character strengths did you ignore or downplay? Do your answers to these questions change how you think about the next steps in your life journey?

CHAPTER 2

VIRTUE AS A WAY FORWARD

Evil consists in injustice, cruelty, and indifference to a neighbor's
trouble, while virtue is brotherly love, goodness, justice,
beneficence, and concern for the welfare of one's neighbor.
— Musonius Rufus, *Discourses*, Lecture 14.9

Virtue is one of those words that seems to have fallen out of
favor, and which people can have a hard time defining. What
does it mean to act virtuously? When asked this question, some
might conjure up a dramatic knight's tale of medieval chivalry,
where virtue is rescuing a damsel in distress. Some might describe
an impossibly pure state of being, an ideal that has no practical
implications. However, as Musonius Rufus makes clear, for Stoics, virtue is excellence in action in everyday life, and the results
benefit everyone, including "one's neighbor."

Musonius Rufus was a first-century Roman born into an aristocratic family. This gave him access to, and influence over, the
Roman Senate and Stoic philosophy, which, since Zeno's time,
had morphed into something much more in line with Roman,
rather than classical Greek, ideals. Despite Musonius' wealth and
social status, his haircut was not fancy or fashionable. Like his
beard, it was of moderate length and kept clean and tidy to protect his skin from sunburn. His clothing was simple and fit for
purpose. It protected him from the elements and maintained his

modesty. Musonius approached diet much the same way. Unlike other Romans of his social class, he shunned exotic gourmet options in favor of local, cheaper fruits and vegetables, which he supplemented with milk, cheese, and honeycombs, but never meat. Everything he did was focused on cultivating good character, a sound mind, and a strong, healthy body. For Stoics, that is what is meant by *virtue* because virtue is to be lived.

In his day job, Musonius was the head of a Stoic school that emphasized that both men and women (despite the gendered norms of the time) should be taught about virtue and the value of philosophy, so that they might become well-rounded citizens and good people. Lessons were designed around sets of mental exercises that helped students achieve personal growth while becoming upstanding members of Roman society. Musonius insisted that philosophical theory should lead to action because, without it, his students could not claim to be honing their virtuous skills, any more than a doctor could claim to heal patients through a physical evaluation alone. In this regard, Stoic philosophy has more in common with medicine or a session with a personal trainer than it does with the university-course model. This is because it is fundamentally about detecting what is right or wrong in a person's approach to life and giving them what they need to get better.

As Musonius Rufus said (as recorded in Epictetus, *Discourses* 3.23.29: "If you have nothing better to do than to praise me, then I am speaking to no purpose."[1] Evidently, Musonius was a man who called a spade a spade. He favored concise practical arguments that were both persuasive and easily understood. He saw no reason to use extravagant language to impress people, and he did not stroke powerful egos. As Musonius wanted people to be better, not just look and feel better, he refused to tell people to "fake it until you make it"[2] because to do so was plain nonsense — cheap sophistry filler that would have charmed the powerful in Rome (who exiled him twice) to the detriment of his virtuous character, moral integrity, and credibility as a teacher.

The four Stoic virtues — courage, justice, self-control, and wisdom — are meant to guide all choices and actions, great and small. In Stoicism, practicing *courage* means consistently, deliberately, and rationally facing dangerous or socially uncomfortable situations in pursuit of noble causes. *Justice* means ensuring that all beings are treated fairly and *self-control* means, among other things, consciously and habitually making the choice to regulate appetites for food, drink, money, and sex. This involves calling out and countering injustice whenever and however it arises. This might mean, for example, attempting to reconcile a workplace disagreement by attentively listening to all parties and carefully examining all sides. Not rushing to take sides or pronounce guilt requires guarding against peer pressure and false impressions that arise from favoritism, seniority, or the relative status of those involved. In a fair process, character is what matters most, and hierarchy and workplace credentials are of secondary importance.

Finally, you are said to be *wise* when you are able to unwaveringly judge what is good, bad, or neither. While deliberating on the workplace disagreement, wisdom would tell you when and how to intervene in a fair and appropriate way. It would enable you to properly examine the evidence, piece together what happened, and determine what is good or bad, right or wrong. Wisdom then guides you to the best actions to take to solve the problem, whether that's by improving communication or tasking the parties involved with agreeing to an effective resolution.

Virtue is not self-proclaimed but rather demonstrated through mindset and actions. Nor is it a way to be or not be depending on circumstances or mood. The contemporary philosopher Christopher Gill's[3] definition of virtue as "a form of knowledge that shapes your whole personality and life" supports this view. Julia Annas, meanwhile, defines virtue as a persistent, reliable feature, tendency, or characteristic that develops in a person as they deliberately respond rationally to challenges and difficulties.[4] Like a muscle, the more a person strives toward virtue, the larger and stronger they will grow and the more effective they will become. Conversely, if a person consistently shies away from facing problems or tackles them poorly, then, as with a muscle, their virtue will diminish.

The Stoics understand virtuous character to be a uniquely human trait that signifies excellence.[5] The Greek term for "excellence" is *arete*, a word that applies to excellence of any kind, even that of inanimate objects. In fact, the standard example is that of the knife, which is deemed excellent if it cuts well, since that is its purpose. Stoics argue that humans are designed to live in harmony with Nature* and one another. As an analogy, consider a simple playground game where all players must do their best to keep a ball up in the air. Stoics would consider the team to be acting with excellence when they work together to ensure that the ball does not touch the ground. This collaborative effort requires a shared understanding that one careless touch or one selfish decision will effectively end the game for all. At the same time, Stoics would say that an individual team member acts with "excellence"

---

* For the Stoics, humans have a self-preservation instinct and a social/communal instinct. Living in harmony with Earth's natural processes is a key component of such living because destroying the environment in which we live is an irrational and antisocial thing to do. A useful analogy is health: Though we might never meet anyone who is perfectly healthy, it is a person's natural state. Doing anything to purposely deteriorate our bodily health for money, social status, or for the mere sake of it is foolish. Likewise, living harmoniously is to be *morally* healthy; that is, wise, just, brave, and temperate.

when performing to the best of their ability. This means that regardless of how well their teammates play, there would never be a reason for any player to put in a half-hearted effort.

Excellence, as understood in this way, leads to *eudaimonia*. While playing a game, virtue is the balance of physique, technique, and mental resilience that players aim for, while the passes of teammates (both the sublime and the wayward) become training exercises for keeping the ball up in the air as long as possible. When applied to the game of life, virtue is not something to put off until the proverbial bedroom is sufficiently tidy. It is the goal for every moment. This highlights why the popular saying "charity begins at home" makes no sense. For one, it is not charity if it is an appropriate action or duty; and second, if something begins at home, that should not mean "stays and ends at home." Why leave the best of yourself at the doorstep? Instead, virtue should be practiced at home and be carried along with you as you go about your day, wherever you are and whoever you are with. It is not something to drop or conveniently forget when life does not go as planned. Nor, for that matter, when life goes so well that being courageous, just, and wise seem unrequired or unnecessary.

Virtue does not exist in a vacuum; it is revealed by our behavior and interactions and relationships with others. Helping strangers, doing our bit for the environment, working on self-improvement, and being successful in the office are not mutually exclusive states. It follows that the manner in which we navigate the world reflects our progress. At first glance, this might seem counterintuitive. But take, for example, two much sought-after states of being: health and wealth. It is normal for humans to choose, all things being equal, good health rather than illness and wealth rather than poverty. No one wants to be sick or to hold a low-paying job, but Stoics remember that such factors have no bearing on their character or their ability to achieve human excellence. This is evidenced by the fact that we can be rich yet morally bankrupt; physically weak yet morally strong. Even being both healthy and wealthy provides no guarantee of fulfillment. Fame does not shield someone from misery, as the suicides and rehabilitations of some of the world's most successful musicians and film stars testify. By contrast, we can be both poor and sick yet find contentment in knowing that our physical condition and present circumstance do not define us nor hinder our journey toward happiness.

The good news is that aiming for virtue, as this chapter explores in detail, although not easy, is completely within our control. It is not subject to anything other than soundness and maturity of mind. This is how Stoicism's founder Zeno could proclaim that the quest for excellence is a journey that all humans can embark on. That's also why Stoics hold that financial wealth, bodily health, geographical location, and social status are simply nonfactors in the journey toward *eudaimonia*. That is not to say that we should be indifferent to external circumstances. In Stoicism, virtue includes speaking up against injustice and greed. At the same time, improving external factors is not the main goal or the end game. Instead, they are the means to our virtuous ends, guiding our choices and behavior, which, of course, impact us, our loved ones, our fellow citizens of the world, and the planet. For evidence of this, let's consider Musonius Rufus' student Epictetus.

Epictetus was born a slave. His birth name, if he was ever given one, is lost to history; the name by which he is known literally means "captured" or "acquired." It was probably assigned to him as he was taken from his home in Hierapolis (modern-day Turkey) and handed to a master in Rome.* The man who bought Epictetus was called Epaphroditus, an ex-slave who did not live

---

* The ancient Stoic view on slavery is nuanced and beyond the scope of this chapter. The ancient Stoics did not call for the outright abolition of slavery as an institution, but they did reflect on how one should strive to treat those in their household with fairness and compassion. See Seneca, *On Clemency* 1:18, for example.

up to his name, which means "lovely." In fact, Epaphroditus received military honors and was rewarded handsomely for supporting the tyrant Emperor Nero in his reign of terror. By the
time Epictetus came to be in Epaphroditus' possession, Epaphroditus was a wealthy landowner who basked in his power and used
brutality to distance himself from his own humble origins. One of
his particularly cruel acts was the violent shattering of Epictetus'
leg, which left the latter with a lifelong limp.[6]

Epictetus' conviction to work toward his self-improvement,
despite his social position and abject poverty, led him, with Epaphroditus' permission, to study Stoicism under Musonius' tute-
lage.[7] In these classes, Epictetus reflected on the moral difference
between those who were slaves due to circumstances of birth and
war and those who were enslaved due to their thirst for wealth,
power, and social status. For Stoics, the bondage of the mind, not
the shackles around the wrists and ankles, is what prevents someone from living what Zeno referred to as the "good life." Thus,
as Epictetus engaged with philosophy, he recognized the importance of liberating his mind from vice, even when legally tied to
a treacherous master. Once Epictetus had learned this, he understood that anyone could be unjust toward him — even kill him —
but that no one could make him a coward. Only he could do that,
if he were to forsake his own principles. Epictetus said (*Discourses*
1.1.23): "Fetter me? You will fetter my leg; but not Zeus himself
can get the better of my free will."

Poverty, physical disability, and even being labeled as property do not prevent us from having a virtuous disposition, any
more than wealth and power prevent us from having a vicious one.
This is why it is the desire to do what is right for the right reasons
that leads to Stoic virtue. Once freed, Epictetus went on to share
this life-changing notion. He became head of his own school of
Stoic philosophy and was revered among his peers. Many of the

Roman elite attended his lessons, such was his reputation. One of them was the Emperor Hadrian. Another was Flavius Arrian, who went on to serve under Hadrian and become a distinguished historian in his own right. It was Arrian's classroom notes that immortalized Epictetus' wisdom. Arrian captures Epictetus' character and powerful prose in the prologue of the *Discourses*:

> Yet to me it is a matter of small concern if I shall be thought incapable of "composing" a work, and to Epictetus of no concern at all if anyone shall despise his words, seeing that even when he uttered them he was clearly aiming at nothing else but to incite the minds of his hearers to the best things. If, now, these words of his should produce that same effect, they would have, I think, just that success which the words of the philosophers ought to have; but if not, let those who read them be assured of this, that when Epictetus himself spoke them, the hearer could not help but feel exactly what Epictetus wanted him to feel.

Epictetus' commitment to excellence did not just benefit the highest echelons of Roman society. In fact, as the early Christian scholar and theologian Origen of Alexandria remarks,[8] Epictetus' teachings were popular among the general public because they were written down by Arrian in Koine Greek, which was the colloquial language of the day.[9] Meanwhile, the works of other philosophers were written in Attic Greek, a very old-fashioned form of the language that, then as now, could only be accessed by the highly educated. Koine Greek — which was also used to write the New Testament — could be understood by both the emperor and the slave and read by those with a more ordinary level of education and status. Therefore, Epictetus' teachings were accessible to all those who sought excellence through the practice of virtue.*

As Epictetus taught, virtue and vice are made manifest in our daily life through the decisions and actions we take. To be courageous, a soldier must demonstrate courage when it is required. Involvement in a battle or the fact of being a soldier per se does not make someone virtuous. Instead, a commitment to virtue will come through in the way that someone serves their fellow soldiers and civilians and how they interact with those considered to be the enemy. It will also manifest in how they use their position to prevent deaths and even war crimes.

The same is true with the things we own, not just our jobs. A father could hardly claim to be virtuous if he spent his family's savings on a car that made him feel better about his midlife crisis. However, that same purchase might be considered virtuous if that new vehicle meant that his family members could get to school, medical appointments, and work — and the price of the car was within the agreed family budget. The car itself is of secondary importance to the way in which it is pursued, obtained, and used. This leads to a very important concept that Stoics refer to as either "externals" or "indifferents." For Stoics, the term *indifferens*, when used as a noun, refers to anything that has no bearing on a person's good character, which is the only thing that truly matters; this is not the adjective *indifferent*, as in not caring or lacking feeling. In the family car example, the car is an indifferent; in itself, it does not reflect the

---

* For Epictetus, just like his mentor Musonius, the importance of oral-lesson scribing was not to create a formally composed work of literature, but instead to help his students in the real world. For these two men, the ability to read and understand the Attic Greek of Plato only mattered in that, as Stoic philosophers and teachers, they could use this ability to guide others in their journey toward virtue.

father's virtue or lack thereof. Rather, his reasons are key, as are his intentions, and the dynamics of the family's situation. If buying a car with family funds only serves himself, this negatively impacts his character. If that same money is spent to help everyone and improve the family's quality of life, then it reflects well on his character. Even buying a cheap car isn't necessarily virtuous if the reasons are inappropriate. Motivations define character.

Stoics are not indifferent, in the common sense of the word, to the way in which people are treated. On the contrary, Stoicism asks us to treat others justly, especially those closest to us — such as a spouse, children, parents, siblings, and so on. Stoics should seek harmony with others, to the extent that such harmony is possible. The ancient Stoics believed that the best way to learn how to act virtuously is to find a role model — one popular role model was the Roman statesman Cato the Younger, whom we will meet in the next chapter. Consider who might be a role model for you. Rather than choose one person, make a short list of people you consider to be particularly courageous, just, self-controlled, and wise. Then ask yourself why you feel each person is a good example. Now, no one is perfect.* No single person could exemplify all the virtues in their every single thought and action. However, take the time to examine and consider those thoughts, attitudes, and acts that do fulfill those criteria, while identifying real-life examples to emulate.

---

* For Stoics, a perfect person is someone who has perfected their character to the point that their thoughts and actions are in complete harmony with the universe. Such persons were referred to as "sages" and thought to be as rare as the phoenix. That said, and the sage aside, no one is truly without flaws, even our role models and heroes. However, we can hold someone up for their great feats in one area of life, and follow their example, while at the same time recognizing their less-than-exemplary behavior in other areas.

When Leo and I were discussing who to place in our short list of contemporary role models, we came up with two seemingly contradictory examples: Pat Tillman, a professional American football player and soldier who died fighting George W. Bush's "War on Terror," and Katharine Gun, a British translator and spy turned whistleblower, who tried to stop the war in Iraq from happening.

Pat Tillman is our role model because he prioritized good character and exemplified good behavior over the trappings of fame and fortune. Although he may not have considered himself a Stoic, and may never have come across the philosophy, his outstanding bravery, unquestionable loyalty, and fair-mindedness are certainly character traits the ancient Stoics valued.

Tillman did not have the build of the typical football player. He was not the fastest nor the biggest. However, he was determined to outwork everyone and give everything of himself to his teammates. His drive for excellence earned him the reputation of a hard hitter with a big heart — traits that promoted him from a late seventh-round draft pick to starting safety for the Arizona Cardinals in week one of the 1998 season. He rewarded the Cardinals' loyalty on the field by helping them reach the playoffs in his rookie year, and in 2000, he had a breakout season that earned him a place in the *Sports Illustrated* All-Pro team. He also repaid the team by turning down a $9.3-million contract offered by the St. Louis Rams, preferring to stay on his rookie salary of $512,000 for another year. Tillman justified his decision by stating that the Cardinals "took a chance on me when no one else would."

The following year, Tillman's commitment to his principles shocked the world of sports again when he turned down the Cardinals' $3.6-million contract offer in favor of enlisting in the US Army. Because of Tillman's superstar status, the army offered him a speaking job that would motivate the troops and keep him out of harm's way. He turned it down. He did not want special treatment. He reasoned that since other people's sons, brothers, and husbands fought in the line of fire, so would he. He toured Iraq in 2003 and then went to Afghanistan in 2004, where he was tragically killed by friendly fire. Tillman's legacy lives on through the foundation that bears his name. It raises funds for military personnel and their spouses who undertake research that empowers others to make the world a better place.[10] Tillman's example shows us how virtuous actions carry a ripple effect that continues even long after we are gone.

Our second role model is Katharine Gun, a British translator who in 2003 leaked a top-secret memo from the US National Security Agency (NSA) because it represented a request for assistance in the blackmailing or bribing of the six nonpermanent UN Security Council members. The idea behind the memo was to swing the vote in favor of a UN resolution that would legalize the Iraq War. Gun was appalled by the idea that dirty tricks were being employed to justify a global act of aggression. She had signed up to the secret service to gather intelligence to protect the British people from acts of terrorism and was proud to work there. However, she objected to gathering intelligence to fix a vote that would deceive the world and exempt the British and American governments from any war crimes committed in Iraq. Her principles told her that she had to act, even if in doing so she would put her job, marriage, freedom, and reputation in jeopardy. She considered such concerns of little consequence compared to playing her part to try to stop an imminent war.

Convinced of the impending injustice, Gun decided to defy her government's desire to go to war by getting a copy of the NSA memo to the press. This made front-page news, and for a fleeting moment it looked like her small act of defiance would be enough.

Unfortunately, an editorial procedure that corrected the article's American spellings into British ones caused media around the world to dismiss the memo as a fake. Britain and America went to war. Gun had failed. To make matters worse, after handing herself in to protect her colleagues from being scrutinized, she was charged with treason.

The case went to trial, where, despite confessing to having printed the memo, Gun pleaded not guilty. She reasoned that treason meant acting against the interests of the British people and that by courageously trying to prevent an illegal war she had done the opposite. The Crown prosecution, acting on behalf of the British government, dropped the charge in the courtroom just as proceedings were about to commence. Gun was free to go. Her legacy lives on in the 2019 film *Official Secrets*. Her example vividly reminds us how an ordinary person committed to virtue can make a difference, even if they fail to achieve what they originally set out to do.

The fact that one of Leo's and my role models fought in the same war that another fought to prevent tells us that war in and of itself is an indifferent. In Stoicism, the person's commitment to virtuous principles is what matters. Despite their vastly different backgrounds, both Pat Tillman and Katharine Gun are exemplary Stoics, in everything but name, because they believed that excellence is pursuing virtue whatever the cost. This is why, if, like Musonius or Epictetus, you decide to use Stoicism to improve your life, you'll need to evaluate why and how you do things, at work, at home, and even on social media. You will need to consider carefully what exactly lies and does not lie in your control. Correctly identifying the difference between the two will give you the power to change how you feel about your life and the courage to address what falls short of the Stoic virtues.

MUSONIUS' QUESTIONS

People often misunderstand what it is that makes them happy. Some people confuse *pleasure* and *comfort* with *happiness*. Some people chase status and money in order to be happy. Others hoard things or focus too much on what others think of them. There is nothing inherently bad (or good) about desiring what is pleasurable or that which makes life easier, unless it starts interfering with your character in a negative way.

- Look around. What is no longer serving you because it is getting in the way of your capacity to think and act virtuously? Is it a possession? If it is, why are you keeping it? Is it a friendship? Is it a job? Why do you value it? Is there a way of making these things work better for yourself and your family?

CHAPTER 3

KNOW WHAT'S IN YOUR CONTROL (AND ISN'T!)

Some things are within our power, while others are not. Within our power are opinion, motivation, desire, aversion, and, in a word, whatever is of our own doing; not within our power are our body, our property, reputation, office, and, in a word, whatever is not of our own doing.
— Epictetus, *Enchiridion* I.I

One of Epictetus' most significant contributions to Stoic philosophy was his development of Aristotle's term *eph' hemin* to distinguish what "is up to us" or "within our power" from what is not.* He used it to highlight the personal benefit of carefully considering, and acting on, what you can control and accepting what you cannot, a concept captured in the phrase *dichotomy of control*.[1] While most people regularly fluctuate between thinking and acting like all things are up to us (everything's our fault) and that everything is beyond our control (nothing's our fault), neither of these two extremes are rational or helpful. Let's say we trip on the doorstep and sprain our ankle. What is a reasonable response? It's true that we are not fully in control of

---

* This concept encapsulates the underlying reason why Zeno, in his utopian book *The Republic*, suggests that anarchy has its uses. Anarchy is not synonymous with chaos; an anarchic mindset implies that no one gets to do our thinking for us. Moreover, it means we don't get to let anyone else make our decisions or take responsibility for them. It's on us, and it's up to us. All of it.

33

the healing process, but there are actions we can take to improve or, conversely, aggravate our condition. Reason holds that we should, at the very least, rest our foot; depending on the severity or longevity of the pain, we might also call a doctor. We are then left with another set of choices. Do we follow the doctor's medical advice or ignore it and risk injuring our ankle further? We also have choices regarding the doorstep. Was it just bad luck to trip and fall or had we tripped less seriously before and knew this was a hazard? Will we, now injured, finally fix what should have been fixed before? Even if our accident was just down to luck, then we still have a sense of control. We can choose how to respond to the potential of having another accident. We might pay more attention to how we leave and enter the house, or we might decide not to give it a second thought. Or we might decide that "the universe is out to get us" and never leave our home again.

In Stoicism, regardless of the specific situation faced, there is no need to be Superman any more than there is a need to be a victim. Both positions tie us to unreasonable expectations, leaving us feeling troubled, frustrated, and anxious.[2] Blaming ourselves for everything that goes wrong exposes us to burnout at the risk of alienating others; congratulating ourselves for everything that goes right, especially when we downplay other people's abilities and their role in helping us reach the top, puts us on a very precarious pedestal. Likewise, passing the buck at the earliest opportunity robs us of moral agency and would stunt our personal growth because we would be consistently shying away from what is worthwhile in favor of what is easy. It would also prevent us from experiencing *eudaimonia*, which is not a product of our circumstances but rather of our ability to transcend them.

While we may not always control the outcome of our actions, we are in control of how we respond to their consequences. This is not to say that we can all be as self-controlled as Zeno or that we won't fall short, even after we have tried to do the right thing. Being Stoic isn't about being perfect or pretending to be something we are not. There is virtue in acknowledging that we don't know something, that we may have misjudged someone, or that we were just plain wrong. There is virtue in owning our mistakes *and* in being comfortable admitting that we are only responsible for *our* mistakes and not someone else's.

A well-known Stoic example that distinguishes what is up to us from what is not comes from a conversation between the Roman senators Cicero and Cato the Younger. They discuss an archer who takes aim at a target and lets their arrow fly.[3] Is actually hitting the target important? Stoics consider the outcome a preferred indifferent; it is not something the archer can control and therefore their happiness should not rest on it. However, if the archer were careless, this would represent a failure on their part to make the right choice, which would be categorized as an "evil." Cato argues that the "good" lies in the archer doing all they can to aim carefully, and this "good" is what Stoics prioritize over everything else. This dialogue illustrates how the capacity to behave virtuously is completely within our control, while worldly success is something that we can influence but not control.

Now, let's apply this to a modern, real-life example using two almost identical archers who stood in almost the same spot, with the same bow and the same strength of conviction, yet achieved vastly different results. The first archer is Rosa Parks, and the second archer is Claudette Colvin, her contemporary, whose similar act of bravery is only just coming to light. Rosa Parks clearly understood the value of knowing what lies within our control. Her target was racial and political justice, which she carefully aimed for but had no guarantee of hitting. Her pulling back on the bow was a courageous act of defiance against the Montgomery bus segregation policies, which mandated that a "colored" person must give up their seat to a white person. By refusing to stand, Parks' arrow struck at the heart of institutionalized racism. Claudette Colvin's arrow, on the other hand, which was fired in March 1955, a full nine months *before* Parks' act of resistance, has all but been forgotten. Colvin was also commuting home when she refused to give up her seat on a Montgomery bus. In her case, she was expected to yield to a young white woman and move, with her two friends, into the aisle so the white woman could sit alone. Like Parks, Colvin refused to obey the driver's orders, was physically dragged from the bus, arrested, and fined. While Colvin's testimony, as the first person to defy Montgomery's racially unjust policies, was integral to the US Supreme Court's later desegregation ruling, her role in the civil rights movement is often overlooked. Indeed, had Parks not also refused to surrender her seat, Colvin's act of resistance might have led to nothing more than her arrest and incarceration. It was Parks, not Colvin, who obtained fame and acclaim for helping set the wheels of desegregation in motion, culminating in the US Congress honoring her as the "first lady of civil rights" and the "mother of the freedom movement."[4] Returning to the Stoic archery analogy, Parks hit the target while Colvin missed through no fault of her own. However, in aiming for excellence, both women did the right thing and their actions were equally virtuous.

Only when we consistently do the right thing for the right reasons do we experience personal growth. Likewise, we only learn the impact of our actions, whether we hit the target or not, after we loose the arrow. When Parks and Colvin refused on separate occasions to stand up on a bus, they couldn't possibly have known whether this small act would make any larger *social* difference. But it made a *moral* difference. This brings us to an interesting thought experiment, which is not so far-fetched considering that both Parks and Colvin went to the church led by Martin Luther King Jr., and they likely knew (or at least knew of) each other. What would have happened if Parks, on hearing about Colvin's defiance and arrest, had decided not to protest because she assumed that the result would be the same: a failed attempt to trigger social change? Since hitting the target is beyond our control, what if Parks had decided not to do the right thing just because it was the right thing to do?

♫♫♫♫♫

Part of understanding what is up to us and what isn't involves identifying what role we can (or currently do) play in addressing any given problem, including those that go beyond ourselves and our immediate family (which most problems do). American football provides an excellent example of how we should approach problems that can only be solved when a whole host of people cooperate. As any fan knows, converting a game-winning field goal is not simply a matter of the kicker's leg connecting with the football. His chance of success is affected by the distance from the goal, the quality of the snap, how high the opponent team jumps, and the weather conditions. All these factors come into play and influence the team's ability to score three points.

With that in mind, every team member will do their bit to get the offense closer to the goal line, so that the kicker has a better chance of making it. Sure, luck plays a part, but effort does, too. Of course, there is always the possibility that a player will mess up or that a gust of wind will carry the ball outside the goalposts. That doesn't mean that the kicker or any other member of the team should not take his training seriously. On the contrary, all players and coaches heavily invest in practicing drills that bring out the team's best performance, regardless of what the opponent or weather does. Team members also sharpen their mental focus for those times when resilience, and not just repetition, gives them the winning edge.

Cato the Younger is perhaps the most notable example of just how deeply you can immerse yourself in Stoic training.⁵ His commitment was so extreme that some Roman Stoics believed that Cato achieved the status of a Stoic "sage," that is to say someone of perfect virtue (supposedly as rare as the phoenix). It is unlikely that Cato would have considered himself to be an ideal Stoic, especially given his temper, but it is true that he went to great lengths to become one. Like Musonius Rufus, Cato was disciplined, and he was determined to use his position as senator and his privilege of birth to achieve virtue.

In living out his commitment to the Stoic virtue of self-control, Cato involved himself in the more arduous tasks required on his farm and didn't leave everything for his slaves to do. He taught himself to endure cold, heat, sickness, and self-imposed poverty without complaint. He trained himself to eat and wear nothing beyond the bare essentials, even though he could well afford luxuries. He occasionally indulged in food and wine at dinner parties, but he did this to more effectively influence the Roman Republic in ways that he considered to be for the common good.*

Not unlike the administrations of many American governments, running the Roman Republic was all too frequently marred by personality politics, questionable electoral practices, and scandal. Not one to pass up on a training exercise, Cato used its trials and tribulations to practice virtue, which often required him to

---

*   Cicero claims that Cato drank socially so he could learn more about Stoicism, a philosophy he embraced not so he could debate or impress people in discussion but so that he might become a good person. See *Pro Murena* 62 for more details.

take a stand against public matters of injustice.* Cato's commitment to his principles, to the ire of his peers, led his fellow senator Cicero to quip (*Epistulae ad Atticum* 2.1.8):

> As for our friend Cato, you do not love him more than I do: but after all, with the very best intentions and the most absolute honesty, he sometimes does harm to the Republic. He speaks and votes as though he were in the Republic of Plato, not in the crap heap of Romulus.

Time after time, Cato showed himself to be above petty politics but not the rule of law. In a world where money talked and gave you a lot of political sway (as it does today), Cato publicly demonstrated that he could not be bought for any price. He also made it clear to his fellow senators, who were among the worst offenders in all of Rome, that he would personally ensure that those involved in corruption would be brought before a jury and, if found guilty, exiled. Unsurprisingly, Cato found himself in an uphill struggle. The most famous case of Cato's failure to prosecute a corrupt official involved the senator Murena. Despite being obviously guilty of bribery, Murena walked away relatively unscathed after he was defended, for political reasons, by Cicero, who cowrote (with Cato) the antibribery laws in the first place! In Cicero's highly hypocritical and improbable defense, he distracted the jury so much that they forgot about Murena's crimes.

---

* Cato was true to the Stoics' position that the sage would take part in politics (if nothing prevents them). However, we must be careful about positing Cato as an exemplar of justice; after all, he fought on the side of the Optimates against the Populares so that the Senate could keep their aristocratic and inherited privileges. While not necessarily an unjust action, this caused injustices to arise. That said, we might give Cato the benefit of the doubt because he felt that the alternative to an aristocracy was a dictatorship, which is, arguably, a less-preferred political system.

He did so by teasing Cato about his character flaws and shortfalls relative to the Stoic ideal. He also, despite having been inspired by Stoicism himself, attacked Cato's moral case by bringing into question Cato's philosophical influence. He achieved this by framing Stoicism as a foreign, and therefore weak, import into Roman culture, which undermined the moral basis of Cato's claims. Tellingly, Cicero begged the jury not to let Cato's dignity, reputation, and commitment to virtue get in the way of a "fair" trial! (See Cicero, *Pro Murena*, for details.) This example shows that even if we act virtuously, which is in our control, there is always the possibility that an unforeseen obstacle will get in our way. How could Cato have ever envisioned that his friend and fellow lawmaker would use his commitment to virtue against him?

Cato's greatest opponent was not Cicero, but another senator, Julius Caesar, who committed a genocidal crime during the Gallic Wars that resulted in the breaking of a truce with the Germanic tribes and the mass murder of noncombatants, including defenseless women and children (see Plutarch's *Cato* 51). Despite the viciousness of Caesar's acts, the entire Senate, except for Cato, refused to condemn Caesar.[6] In fact, they hailed him for his heroics! This went against everything Cato stood for and led him to publicly call out Caesar's victory brag. This courageous act set the stage for Cato's armed opposition against Caesar during the Roman Republic's civil war (which involved a big chunk of Europe, Asia Minor, and North Africa). Although war is never a reasonable person's first choice, Cato felt he could not avoid it. After all, it was his moral duty to prevent Rome from becoming a tyrannical dictatorship,[7] which also meant that it was his prerogative to stop Caesar from bringing the Republic to its knees.

Cato was a brave and capable man of the military who, in sharp contrast to the brazen Caesar, went about his work modestly and quietly. He made sure that he used daily hardships to master his own mind. Even when on leave from his soldiering duties, as a tribune in Macedon, he eschewed luxurious destinations to attend the lectures of renowned Stoic philosophers. In this sense, and similarly to Pat Tillman, the American football player who renounced a life of fame and wealth to serve his nation, Cato understood that his physique and social position made him not just a useful soldier but an inspirational example to his fellow men. He slept on the ground with his foot soldiers, wore what they wore, ate what they ate, and refused to ride on horseback, marching instead alongside them. His comfort lay not in material pleasures but in the wisdom that he gained, which he used to convince his men to do the right thing when they failed in their duties to Rome or to one another. For Cato, the force of reason was more effective in instilling virtue than the wanton use of the lash, which he felt brought out fear instead of the best in people.

Cato's last stand against Julius Caesar was in Utica, located in modern-day Tunisia, during the Roman civil war of 49–45 BCE. Utica was a port city and rendezvous point for the Optimates, who had been squeezed out of Europe by Caesar and his allies, the Populares. Cato and his men arrived in Utica following a thirty-day march through five hundred miles of North African desert (according to Strabo, *Geographica* 27.30). In various meetings with the Roman consul and military commander, Metellus Scipio, it became clear that political tensions in the city were high, and there were conflicting priorities and strategies about how best to stop Caesar. It was ultimately decided that Scipio would face Caesar and his men at what became known as the Battle of Thapsus. Cato advised Scipio to stand firm but not engage. He felt the war could be won by forcing Caesar to conduct a lengthy siege. Cato reasoned that Caesar's men would tire quickly without supplies. By wearing the enemy down, a tactic that would also give the Optimates time to regroup, it might also be possible to reverse the Optimates' fortunes. However, Scipio didn't listen. He was convinced that playing the long game was unnecessary. Drunk on the glory he thought his heroics would bring him, he launched a full attack. Caesar not only outmaneuvered him, he crushed his forces. Scipio escaped but many of his men didn't. The few that managed to reach the stronghold back at Utica convinced Cato that the situation was dire and that it was only a matter of time before Caesar would show up and demand they surrender.

Upon hearing this news, and holding fast to his principles, Cato gathered together his remaining forces, told them that defeat and Caesar's dictatorship was imminent, thanked them, and invited them to wisely choose their next course of action for the good of their families. He then oversaw a letter that asked Caesar to spare the lives of his loyal followers and sent the unspent money tied to his war campaign back to Rome. Never one to be accused of embezzlement, he wanted the virtue of his deeds to remain after he had gone.

For his part, Caesar enjoyed lauding his acts of politically motivated clemency over his enemies, so he would have loved to have pardoned Cato, who was seen as the opposing side's moral figurehead. Cato knew this but preferred suicide in accord with Stoic philosophy (not unlike Socrates who drank hemlock rather than beg for forgiveness from his Athenian jurors).* In conscientious objection to Julius Caesar's power grab and his forthcoming reign of tyranny, which would convert Rome from a republic into

---

* Controversially, in Stoic philosophy, suicide is considered appropriate if it is done as an act of virtue. It should never be done whimsically, out of cowardice, or for trivial matters. For example, it takes courage for a climber to cut their own rope to save the group, or for a parent to push their child out of the way of an oncoming car knowing they themselves could die. A contemporary Stoic example that demonstrates this principle is Vice Admiral James Stockdale who, during the Vietnam War, preferred suicide (and attempted it) to giving incriminating evidence against his fellow prisoners of war under torture.

a dictatorship, Cato disemboweled himself. In death, Cato became immortalized as the archetypal Stoic hero who chooses character over continued existence. Above all things, Cato's greatest ambition was to make the men under his command more like himself.[8] This is why, day after day, he showed everyone he came across that Stoic principles are useless unless they are put into practice for the common good — regardless of whether you are helping out at home, working for political change, or dying beside your brothers and sisters in arms.

Just like Cato, all of us should put our best foot forward because that's what puts us in a position to make a difference. The better prepared we are, the more likely we are to make that difference. That does not mean that focusing on what lies within our control is easy. Sometimes it is very difficult. Other times it is practically impossible. Stoicism invites us to try in any case. Stoicism asks us "to give it our best shot."

My grandad, Eddie, used that very saying to instill the importance of doing your best and being the best form of yourself, even if you failed by some external standard, whether that be on a school test or on the sports field. To motivate me and my siblings (and my mum and her siblings before that), Eddie almost always offered us the chance to win loose change (which he affectionately referred to as a "couple of coppers") to spend on sweets or put toward a toy. However, none of Eddie's prizes were guaranteed. You didn't have to win the race or get top marks to be rewarded, but he didn't give you anything for merely taking part. What he wanted was to know that, like a good archer, you had given your best effort to hit your target. What were you aiming for? Had you tried to succeed, or did you not even aim at all? He would jiggle his trouser pocket while asking questions designed to check how hard my sisters and I had trained for a sports event or studied for an exam. He wanted us to hold ourselves accountable; not for his benefit but for ours.

Eddie's example continues to rub off on me. He exemplified

Epictetus' concept about the dichotomy of control, which is really about consistently grabbing a quiver of arrows, lining up in the right place, and giving it your best shot. In Stoicism, whether people notice you or not, you continue to try because the probability of hitting the target increases every time you choose to do the right thing. Virtue is about doing all you can to push the odds in your favor, even if, like Cato, you ultimately fail.

CATO'S QUESTIONS

Working in the Roman Senate was something Cato believed he was born to do. It wasn't always easy, though, especially when his friend Cicero sided against him in favor of the unjust. However, Cato wasn't deterred in doing what he thought was right because no one could force him to break his Stoic principles.

- Do you have any regrets about a time where you could have been braver or spoken out about something unjust but didn't? What would you do differently now? Which aspects of Stoicism lead you to think differently about how you might approach challenges in the future?

- How would you deal with a situation where following your principles might prevent you from being considered a good team player? What factors would influence your decision? What lies within your control? What does not?

CHAPTER 4

RECOGNIZE LUCK

Lead me Zeus, and thou O Destiny.
Lead me wherever your laws assign me....
Fate guides the willing but drags the unwilling.
— Cleanthes, *The Hymn to Zeus*[1]

I magine a stroke of good fortune, something unexpected that changes your life for the better. What comes to mind? Perhaps winning the lottery or a serendipitous meeting — at summer camp, say, or a company retreat — with the person who ends up being your spouse. Now imagine a stroke of bad fortune. Perhaps you wake up late, get stuck in traffic, and subsequently miss an interview for a dream job that goes to someone else. Upon returning home maybe you begin to curse your bad luck and bitterly complain about how unfair and terrible life is. However, for the ancient Stoics, it made no sense to act this way. For them, the concept of luck or chance, as we generally understand it today, did not exist. Instead, they believed that nothing is truly random but rather the unfolding of cause and effect, as part of the natural order of things.

Taking this perspective prevents us from lingering on what we perceive to be a problem and refocuses our attention on acceptance and *problem solving*. This allows for a much more productive inner conversation because it leads to questions like,

"Can I reschedule the interview for later in the afternoon?" Or, "Is there a friend I can call for advice?" Or even, "Should I buy an analog alarm clock as a backup?" and, "What other jobs can I apply for?" These kinds of questions align our response with fate. Whining does not. Furthermore, our acceptance of the situation gives us the mental space we will need if we are to walk alongside fate, instead of being dragged by it, as this frequently used Stoic metaphor illustrates:

> When a dog is tied to a cart, if it wants to follow, it is pulled and follows, making its spontaneous act coincide with necessity. But if the dog does not follow, it will be compelled in any case. So it is with men [and women] too: even if they don't want to, they will be compelled to follow what is destined.[2]

Sadly, this quote has often encouraged people newly interested in Stoicism to take to social media and declare, for example, that minorities should learn "to embrace the suck" because there is "nothing we can do." This form of reasoning suggests that we should resign ourselves to, or even accept, a whole host of social injustices because "to protest is un-Stoic." However, such reasoning is deeply flawed and its consequences deeply troubling. The Stoics called for *apatheia*, not apathy. While the English term means a "lack of concern," the Greek term has nothing to do with ignoring our own or someone else's plight. It instead encompasses the serene state of mind that is achieved when we accept and even love our destiny. Moreover, all Stoics have the moral obligation to strive toward *eudaimonia* — a journey that requires them to harmoniously seek to improve their character and to do their best to ensure that virtue, which includes justice, is made manifest in their thoughts and actions. This is, as we've discussed, fundamentally about understanding what to do, when to do it, and how best to accomplish it.

While it is true that complaining and wallowing in self-pity is fundamentally un-Stoic, taking action to solve a problem, say by joining a protest in the face of vice, is one of many possible Stoic responses. After all, it is just as unreasonable (and unhelpful) to accept an unjust societal situation — treating it as an insurmountable mountain when it can in fact be climbed and changed — as it is to curse your luck and try to bargain with the universe when a literal mountain blocks your way. As contemporary philosopher Alain de Botton explains when discussing the Stoic cart:

> We can as easily go astray by accepting the unnecessary and denying the possible, as by denying the necessary and wishing, for the impossible. It is for reason to make the distinction.[3]

With reason, we can sketch out the likely path the cart we are tied to is going to take and the obstacles it is likely to meet. Calculating our trajectory in this way means that we are less likely to be shocked or jolted by what others might perceive as a sudden change of direction or an abrupt stop. In this regard, Stoicism occupies the middle ground between "destiny is completely determined by a causal chain" and "destiny is formed at random." Returning to the cart metaphor, we can capture the Stoic perspective on fate by considering the degree of freedom offered by the length of the rope that ties us to the cart and the fact that reason allows us to determine how much slack we have at any given moment. We may not be able to stop the cart or make it change direction, but we do have some choices available to us. We can, for instance, decide which loose stones and boulders to step on or over. Sometimes that's enough. This reality is encapsulated by what Cicero called (in Stoic Paradoxes 5.34) "the power to live what you will."

In this sense, what comes about through fate comes about *through you*, which means that you must acknowledge a sense of responsibility for what happens to you, as far as what happens is up to you. When you take the time to scout the horizon for opportunities, you will succeed where others fail because you will have given yourself time to react, to redirect, and to brace yourself for the bump or rut in the road. You will succeed not just, or not necessarily, because you are more talented than someone else but because you are doing all you can to push the odds in your favor.

Cleanthes, the man who penned the hymn to Zeus that opens this chapter, is a prime example of a Stoic walking the middle ground. Another Stoic immigrant, this time from Assos (in what is now modern-day Turkey), he was not what most people have in mind when they imagine a world-leading philosopher. For one thing, he was a former boxer and probably had a broken nose, knuckle-busted hands, and cauliflower ears to boot.[4] The ancient form of boxing was brutal. There were no weight classes, no ring, and judging from classical Greek artwork, a preference for attacking the face.

Given the prevalence of long-term boxing-related injuries and disabilities, it is more than likely that the slow-wittedness that characterized Cleanthes' behavior was caused by violent bouts, which ended when the blood was pouring so badly that he reluctantly lifted his finger to signify he could take no more — or when he was hit so hard he was unable to get back up. Even when Cleanthes wasn't boxing, life was hard. When his fellow philosophy students were playing, he was tilling barren ground. While they were sleeping, he was busy with backbreaking late-night odd jobs, including carrying water from wells to the homes of rich people.

Cleanthes' scarce income paid for his day's lectures but bought him little in the way of comfort. This led him to dress in a simple rough cloak with nothing, not even a tunic, underneath. Rather than feeling down because he could not afford papyrus (which was then a very expensive commodity), he focused on what was available to him — pottery shards and cattle bones — and scratched out Zeno's words of wisdom on those. Cleanthes' lack of suitable writing material did not stop him from succeeding. In fact, he was renowned for his discipline, diligence, and faithfulness to Stoic doctrine, qualities that led Zeno to name him, against all odds, as the next head of his philosophical school. These merits also led him to author many books, including *On Time*, *On Marriage*, *On Art*, and *On Natural Ability* — all of which have unfortunately disappeared. It is a real shame that the latter title, in particular, is lost because it would have given us real insight into how to succeed when others around you believe that you have no discernible talent. In fact, many philosophers of the period poked fun at Cleanthes by suggesting that he was so slow and stodgy that he might as well be dead![5] Even Cleanthes' fellow Stoics remarked on his painfully slow way of thinking. Many of them affectionately referred to him as "the Donkey." Rather than get angry with those who mocked him (his fellow Stoics in a friendly manner, others not so), he embraced his nickname, taking it to imply that, like a donkey, he alone could carry the burden of teaching Zeno's principles to the next generation of Stoics. In other words, Cleanthes accepted his various intellectual difficulties, brought on by a life of poverty, fights ending in concussion, and physical toil. He understood the role of luck in his life and played the few good cards he had been dealt to the best of his ability. He was an example of a person who was tied to a very heavy cart with a relatively short leash. Yet he was also a leader who, despite his few degrees of freedom, managed to surpass everyone's expectations (except Zeno's, but perhaps his own).

The short distance between the cart and Cleanthes' neck brings us to an important point. We must not cheapen Stoic teachings by dismissing what is obvious: No two people have equal access to the same type or number of opportunities. It is disingenuous to think otherwise or to take the ancient Stoics to mean that everybody's leash is the same length or that all carts carry the same load. Life is not a level playing field. Thus, it would be unfair and patronizing to suggest that Cleanthes or Epictetus, whose paths were not smooth, might have accomplished as much as the more fortunate ancient Stoics, such as Cato, Seneca, and Emperor Marcus Aurelius, if they had only tried harder.

As college professors, Leo and I are aware that some students in our classes carry a whole host of burdens and heavy baggage, while others arrive tied to the equivalent of a well-oiled carbon-fiber cart. Our role is to help our students to progress and succeed, but that involves more than giving assignments and grading papers. Obviously, a top grade is a top grade, regardless of who hands the paper in, and we must, as professionals and practicing Stoics, be just with our red pen (or these days, our Excel spreadsheet). However, for students who truly need help, we provide it when and if we can, within reason. The beauty of Stoicism is that, when we must decide the best course of action, the emphasis is on using better judgment, not strictly following a rule-based system. For students who speed along with little effort, we might choose to simply move out of the way and shake hands with them at the finish line. For others, we might listen to their troubles and offer advice without direct intervention. Then, at other times, we might get more actively involved, metaphorically putting the brakes on a student's heavy-laden cart before it tumbles off a cliff or leaning our shoulders to the wheel to push it out of a rut.

Of course, when deciding what we will do, it makes a difference if our students are giving their best effort. We both have our fair share of students who believe that everything that doesn't go their way is someone else's fault (often the teacher's). Leo has had students who have complained that they suffer hearing loss from working at nightclubs and thus cannot clearly hear his lectures, which is the reason they give for not doing well in class. An army veteran who has served in Iraq, Leo is no stranger to hearing-loss issues, and if students are genuinely struggling to overcome physical limitations, he may offer sympathetic support. Yet if those same students also come late to class, sit in the back row, spend the entire time glued to whatever is happening on their phone, and fail to do the requested readings — which would be especially important if hearing damage was affecting their learning! — then Leo might instead point out that their behavior is inconsistent with their desire for good grades. Difficult circumstances demand more effort, not less.

From a Stoic perspective, regardless of circumstances, we must always strive to make the right judgments, hold the right beliefs, and take the right actions. At the same time, Stoics believe that no one is deserving of all their successes nor responsible for all their failings. There will be times when a leash feels exceedingly short and the terrain exceptionally difficult. On other occasions, there will be sufficient slack for the beginnings of better choices and better outcomes. Sometimes success really is a matter of being the right person in the right place at the right time. For example, you might be buying your first home just before an unforeseen housing market boom, leading to an unexpected financial windfall. Yet two years later, the same decision to buy a first home could result in financial hardship. At the height of the real estate bubble, you would likely pay more, and have to take out a bigger mortgage, for the same home, and if the bubble collapses soon afterward, your home might drop in value so much it wouldn't be worth what you paid! The same decision taken just two years apart can lead to vastly different outcomes, and these outcomes could affect the rest of your life. In one, you accumulate more wealth, which could be passed on to the next generation, giving them a better start in life. In the other, you accumulate more debt and a heavier cart. Fortune is a fickle thing — it's only right that we acknowledge its existence, especially as there are some things in life that we get praised or blamed for over which we have no or little control.

The ancient Stoics took what we call "luck" to be divine providence, and therefore they saw it as something that was destined but which could not have been foreseen or changed. In one sense, luck refers to the circumstances that lie outside our control. Our choices, intentions, and effort are within our control, but what we achieve with them often is not. Neither fortune nor misfortune may be directly related to our own personal failures or successes. Once we understand luck in this way, we begin to judge ourselves less, both in positive and negative ways. The trials, tribulations, and achievements of life are seen in a different light. The lottery of birth, for instance, makes it much more difficult for women to become professional athletes, and to be paid like male sports stars, even if they train just as hard and win on the field just as much. If we, as a society, want this to be different, we can work together to change the circumstances that foster this inequality, but until then, it might be that, as individuals, we have to accept "that's just the way things are." This same reasoning and dynamic explain why the elite members of Roman and Greek society owned slaves and thought little or nothing of it. Even if an individual recognized slavery as morally wrong, this usually led to them choosing to treat their slaves better — as the ancient Stoics did. This recognition seldom led them to avoid owning slaves or to protest the institution, which was "just the way things are."

Many, maybe most, aspects of life are beyond an individual's control, and yet there can be much we wish were different. Take modern fashion and the clothing industry, much of which depends on slave, child, and unregulated labor. If we are upset over the ethics of clothing production, we can choose to boycott brands, protest, and monitor our own purchases, but this alone won't change the industry or the global economy. That's not to say that efforts to make a difference aren't worth it. As we've discussed, we have a *moral* obligation to carefully consider what lies within our control and to act accordingly. That said, it is equally important to recognize that similar circumstances affect everyone in different ways. In short, we must remember that, at least in some respects, luck determines the difference between what we are able to do and what we would like to do, and the same holds true for everybody.

꒥꒥꒥꒥꒥

For the Stoics, fortune, both good and bad, like just about everything else, is an opportunity to build character. We don't often develop good character when, as contemporary Stoic practitioner Chris Fisher points out, the seas of our life are smooth and the winds are calm and steady, blowing in the direction of our desires. On the contrary, only when the sea swirls and a storm erupts are we suddenly afforded an opportunity to learn how to avoid the rocks. Once we come to grips with that truth, fortune ceases to be the enemy and becomes our guide.[6]

It is worth remembering that Stoics believe that what comes about through fate comes about *through* you and not against you. This means that although our actions are determined in the sense of being a product of preceding causes, they are not forced upon us by others or by God or, indeed, the universe. Consequently, we are able to act as we choose, under our own volition. In other words, we contribute to our own destiny, and we are under no compulsion to take action or refuse to take it.*

The most clear-cut understanding of how the ancient Stoics viewed fate is given by Chrysippus of Soli, a student of, and the successor to, Cleanthes. Like his mentor, Chrysippus was into sports, albeit he was a slim long-distance runner rather than a thickset boxer. He was so important to Stoicism that it is said that the school would never have achieved the recognition it did if he had not existed.[7] This is perhaps not surprising given that Chrysippus was a particularly eager writer, responsible for over seven hundred books (which, like those of Cleanthes, were unfortunately lost to history).

When thinking about how our character and present circumstances intersect to form our fate, Chrysippus argued that our actions and decisions are like a cylinder, which does not roll merely because it can. While its cylindrical form makes a rolling motion possible, that does not mean that it *will* roll. For that to happen it must be placed on a sloped surface or pushed. Thus, the combination of the cylinder's shape, which makes it conducive to rolling, and external factors, such as a sloped environment, cause it to move. The cylinder represents our character; the slope or push represents our circumstances. Chrysippus' metaphor demonstrates that while we can be stimulated or influenced by others and our surroundings (either pushed or placed on a slope), the way we respond depends on our character. In this respect, it is un-Stoic to assume that we are truly slaves to anything or anybody (even

---

*   This tricky Stoic concept is well explained by contemporary philosopher John Sellars in his book *Hellenistic Philosophy* (Oxford, UK: Oxford University Press, 2018), in which he says: "It may be that I will not, and cannot act other than I do. Yet the act is still mine...and not forced upon me."

if they happen to own us or our time). On the contrary, it is very Stoic to believe that no matter how dire our situation, it does not have to define us.

The Italian Formula One and North American Champ Car driver Alex Zanardi is an exemplary case of how character, built over decades, can defy even the strongest winds of fortune, which certainly waxed and waned throughout his career. In 1997 and 1998, Zanardi dominated the Champ Car series.[8] By any standard, he was on top of the world. In 1999, he was invited by Frank Williams to come back to Formula One and drive for what was then a prestigious team. It was an ill-fated return and a disappointing campaign, during which he failed to score a single point. By the end of the season, Zanardi was out of a contract and out of a job. It was tough times for a driver who had proven that he had the talent and strength of character to lead races and win championships.

However, sitting out for an entire year was not the worst thing that awaited Zanardi. In retrospect, you could even say that being unemployed for two seasons would have been better than what happened to him on his return to Champ Cars in 2001, which did not go as planned. His new car was relatively uncompetitive, and the team's best performances were those led by his teammate, who achieved the team's only place on the podium.

Zanardi's biggest chance to show the world that he still had what it took to succeed came on September 15, 2001, at the Euro-Speedway Lausitz circuit in Germany. It was a strange race in many respects, not least because Americans were mourning the tragic events of the 9/11 terrorist attacks that had occurred only four days earlier. Many people believed that it should not have gone ahead. Even the rain seemed to concur, and the organizers took the unusual step of withholding a qualifying session on a track that did not want to dry. This meant that the starting grid was decided by current position in the driver's championship. In 1998 Zanardi would have lined up at the pole position. In 2001, he lined up dead last. Sitting at the back of the grid, he knew the odds of winning the race were slim. But they weren't zero. After all, wasn't he the same driver who had won championships? Hadn't he been steadfast in his training? Hadn't the ups and downs been the grindstone of his character? When the lights went out, he pressed the gas pedal down hard, bringing the engine to full throttle. In a blistering and audacious performance, he passed every competitor and emerged as the race leader. On lap 123, with just twelve to go, he entered the pits on a routine stop, in the full belief that the hardest part was now behind him. He couldn't have been more wrong.

On exiting the pits and rejoining the race circuit, Zanardi's wheels slid on a patch of grass, spinning the car momentarily into a weird angle and putting his body at direct risk of being hit by an oncoming car. Indeed, Alexandre Tagliani plowed straight into him at a speed of more than 200 mph. Zanardi's car was literally torn in two and his legs were severed from his body. It was a freak accident, an act of the gods. No one else had ever been struck in that way. By the time the rescue team got Zanardi out of the cockpit, he was down to one liter of blood. His heart stopped seven times, and the hospital staff put him in a medically induced coma in the scant hope that this would protect his broken body from organ failure. The odds were stacked against him. No one had ever survived a motor racing accident that severe. Unlucky was an understatement. Yet by nothing short of what some people might call a miracle, Zanardi survived, his mind intact.[9]

Once he was over the worst, and the pain-relieving medication had been reduced to a level where he could begin to think,

Zanardi asked himself a difficult question: "How will I do all the things I still want to do without my legs?" The first goal he aimed for was visiting the bathroom unaided, but as he recovered, Zanardi's goals got bigger.[10] Eventually, he wanted nothing more than to get back into the driver's seat. He wanted to feel the excitement of the race. Furthermore, he was convinced that it was his mindset, his character, and not his legs that made him a driver. It was his never-say-die attitude combined with a good car that had led him to victory. He reasoned that he would make his own luck because a life at home and not behind a wheel was, for him at least, not a life worth living.

Ill as he was, Zanardi decided that, if the circumstances weren't favorable, then he would do what he could to make them so. If he had no legs, then he would drive a car that didn't require them. If that was not possible, then he would wear prosthetics that would allow him to accelerate, brake, and change gears. If those prosthetics did not exist, then he would design and make prototypes of his own. In the end, he did all these things. Two years later, using prosthetic legs, he went back to the circuit where he had survived his horrific accident and finished the remaining laps to the roar of the crowd. Two years after that, he won a World Touring Car Championship race, becoming the first disabled driver to win a professional race against not just able-bodied competitors but some of the best in the profession. Zanardi did not stop there. In 2018, as a member of a team competing in North America's most prestigious twenty-four-hour endurance race at Daytona, Florida, he raced a modified BMW, which he could completely control with his hands. Outside of motorsport, he become a Paralympian gold medalist in handcycling and twice set a handcycling world record during an Ironman triathlon.

In 2020, Zanardi's luck turned again. In preparation for the defense of his Olympic title, his handbike crashed into an oncoming truck. Witnesses and medical doctors were surprised that he survived, given the severity of his wounds. Once again, he was placed in an induced coma as doctors worked to save his life, and still today, as Leo and I write this, Zanardi's long-term prognosis remains unclear. However, we are confident that, so long as he has life, Zanardi won't give up.

Zanardi's story goes to show that character is the only guarantee you have of succeeding in life, and that strength of character matters most when the odds are stacked against you. The same can be said for Cleanthes, who, on his way to succeeding Zeno as the head of the Stoa, had to overcome poverty, the damage dealt by bare-knuckled boxing, and the fact that many of his peers mocked his humble background. At the same time, he was lucky to have met Zeno, an older and wiser man who saw past his broken nose and cauliflower ears. However, Cleanthes didn't just ride his luck. Instead, he recognized just how fickle luck can be and willingly sacrificed and toiled away for his education. He was also sufficiently steadfast and thick-skinned to take the slow but necessary steps to become the unlikely leader of one of Greece's most prominent philosophical schools.

Cleanthes' reality is one of the many Chrysippus must have had in mind when he introduced his cylinder analogy to explain the relationship between our character, our circumstances, and what happens to us. Chrysippus' teachings allow us to understand that while we may not always know what opportunities or challenges the future holds, we can always work on sculpting our character. And consequently, the more we invest in its shaping, the better prepared we will be to make the most of our circumstances and ride the downhill momentum when the push finally comes. Yes, luck matters, but how we respond matters more. This is the nature of life. This is Stoicism in action.

CLEANTHES' QUESTIONS

To be a good boxer you need to train hard and eat well. This takes a lot of discipline, especially if your training involves lifting heavy goods for a little extra money instead of sparring with friends. At the same time, whether or not you land the knockout blow, there is always an element of luck involved. Perhaps your opponent tries to duck his head, only to inadvertently receive the full force of your knuckles. Sometimes, you slip on your own sweat as you swing your arm and your opponent's punch causes you to lose your tooth instead.

- Ask yourself how much of your social status, wealth, and health have been an accident of destiny. How much of it have you really been responsible for?

- Do you ever catch yourself believing that you deserve all the pleasant things in your life, yet none of the unpleasant ones? When unpleasant things happen to strangers, do you feel the same way?

CHAPTER 5

NO ONE
IS AN ISLAND

No one, whether a general in war or a leading statesperson at home,
could have accomplished deeds of great service without the support
of his fellow human beings. Their great achievements would
not have been possible without the cooperation of others.
— Panaetius of Rhodes, as quoted by Cicero, *De Officiis* 2.16

Panaetius of Rhodes' words shatter one of the more pervasive,
persistent, and pernicious myths known to humankind: that
of "the self-made man." The myth holds that certain people, usually men, are able to achieve success entirely through their own
individual efforts, with the help of no one else, as if they were an
island cut off from the rest of the world. The moral of this story is
that these people deserve every dollar, business opportunity, and
tax break that comes their way, since they have only their own
remarkable intelligence, talent, and work ethic to thank for their
wealth and achievements. Further, they should be rewarded with
even more money and privileges because they know how to use
them more efficiently than other people who are less deserving or
will only "waste" them.

As stories go, "the self-made man" has been used to extra-
ordinary effect. While this story does not ring true for athletes,
doctors, nurses, teachers, paramedics, firefighters, police officers,
military personnel, and just about everyone who recognizes the
power of team spirit and collaborative efforts, it has often struck

a chord with many of the world's CEOs, entrepreneurs, and politicians. Many people find this myth brings them comfort, hope, and a sense of purpose, since it justifies good fortune by framing it as personally earned and gives the impression that any misfortune will be overcome through personal effort. This, as we saw last chapter, is not the Stoic perspective and certainly not supported by facts. However, even those most detrimentally affected by the myth's message can be enchanted by it.

Why? Because this myth performs a good sleight of hand that moves attention away from a much less-inspiring reality. In fact, approximately one-third of the world's wealthiest people inherited all, or a large proportion of, their riches, and three American dynasties (the Waltons, Kochs, and Marses) own more than the combined fortune of four million hard-working American families.[1] Even though the Wealth-X report[2] bestows the "self-made" title on 68 percent of high-net-worth individuals (on the grounds that they did not inherit a ton of money), the claim that anyone makes it by themselves is incredibly dubious. What it implies is that, if a person is responsible for everything they have obtained, including every penny in their pocket, they aren't obliged to share their wealth with anybody, precisely because they have no one else to thank. We should all be very wary of any such claim or any shiny "self-made billionaire" labels placed on anyone's chest. Is there truly any businessperson who has personally made all of the products their company sells? Did they design the factory and build the roads that allow both their employees to get to work and their products to reach the customer? And how much of a multi-millionaire's or billionaire's net worth comes, not from goods and services created, but from company shares that are floated on a stock market, which they did not create?

No one is self-made. No one is an island completely separated from all others. In fact, wealth and fame (and consequently poverty and anonymity) overwhelmingly derive from the attitudes, thoughts, and actions of others.[3] This is why the Stoics argue that while money and fame may give us pleasure, they don't ultimately lead us to *eudaimonia*. Further, the notion of being "self-made" violates the Stoic lessons that (a) *everyone* is in control of their own attitudes, thoughts, and actions, and (b) outside of making the right judgments, holding the right beliefs, and taking the right actions, *no one* is deserving of all their success nor responsible for all their failings. In short, anyone who claims to be "self-made" can only maintain this illusion if they are willing to ignore the role of luck, including the fact that, through no fault of their own, they have accrued advantages that are simply not available to everyone. No matter how commercially astute and hard-working someone is, no one can make a billion dollars without access to high education levels, innovative technologies, adequate infrastructure, stable economies and societies, and mass-market opportunities. Without these fortuitous circumstances, most of today's top entrepreneurs would probably have had to exhibit their commercial prowess by selling fresh fruit on the side of a dusty road.

When Panaetius of Rhodes reminded his listeners that *no one is an island*, that all our achievements depend on others, he was not a poor man admonishing the rich. He did not write these words as a revolutionary sound bite. He was not an angry farmer with a pitchfork, nor a student activist with a point to prove. He did not wish to galvanize the masses to stand up against the elite. In fact, Panaetius was a member of the upper echelons of the elite. He belonged to a prestigious family of considerable political and religious authority, who also enjoyed social celebrity. Among his ancestors and peers were military generals, athletes, and priests. His grandfather, also called Panaetius, had been one of Poseidon's priests at a temple in Rhodes.[4] This was an incredibly important

position, as the seafaring god played a vital role in bringing fortune, and not disaster, from the waters that lapped the shores of
the Greek mainland and its many islands.

Panaetius' wealth and prestige offered him many opportunities
for travel and scholarship. On one such trip he sailed to Athens.
Here he took his first lessons in Stoicism with Diogenes of Babylon,
then the head of the Stoic school, and with Diogenes' successor,
Antipater of Tarsus. However, it was not just philosophy that the
young and ambitious Panaetius was interested in. He was acutely
aware that the extent of his success and influence depended on the
strength of his social and political alliances. So when he wasn't in
the classroom, he was busy demonstrating his value to the Athenians, who came to like him so much that they asked him to be their
political ambassador to his home island of Rhodes.

Panaetius' most important friendship was with Scipio Aemil-
ianus (also known as Scipio Africanus Minor), a well-regarded
Roman general and top-ranking politician of the Roman Republic, who was at the heart of the Scipionic Circle. The latter was an
exclusive writers' group that only opened its membership to the
most highly regarded intellectuals of the day. Panaetius' aristocratic outlook, paternalistic attitude, and his desire to disseminate
Greek philosophical ideas (albeit with a distinctly Roman flavor)
made him an obvious fit.* His affiliation with the group further
cemented his reputation and influence, and it proved to be the
perfect vehicle for the introduction and proliferation of Stoicism
into Roman society, particularly among Rome's elite. It would
also help him to become recognized as the Stoic school's seventh
leader in 129 BCE.

---

*   Other members included Polybius, who was one of the most highly in-
     fluential historians of all time; the playwright Terence (also known as
     Publius Terentius Afer), who was, despite being brought to Rome as a
     slave, particularly well regarded by Europeans in the Middle Ages and the
     Renaissance; and another Stoic philosopher called Quintus Aelius Tubero.

Many inside the Scipionic Circle became interested in using Stoicism because they were particularly taken by Panaetius' pragmatic approach, which emphasized the need to think and act appropriately. It also simplified the more cumbersome aspects of the Stoic training program, which included formal logic, epistemology, Stoic physics (the study of how the world works), and various other deeply philosophical concerns that had intrigued Panaetius' predecessors, Cleanthes, Chrysippus, and Zeno of Citium.

Panaetius established the Stoic idea that everyone has four roles. The first and primary role is given to us by the virtue of being a rational human being, that is, someone who is able to reason; it is universal to everyone.* The second is shaped by our individual nature: our likes, dislikes, personality traits, and odd quirks. The third is dependent on our personal circumstances, which include where we were born, where we now live, whether we have children or elderly parents, and how much money or social influence we have. The fourth relates to the professional path we wish to take in life. It includes our career choices, the job that we are trained to do, and the corresponding knowledge that we acquire. All four roles combine to determine our moral obligations, responsibilities, and the steps we will take in our journey toward *eudaimonia*. For example, our ability, and therefore our personal obligation, to save lives if we happen to be a motor mechanic will be different from that of a trained doctor. Likewise, our ability, and therefore our personal obligation, to enact legal change will be different for those who are qualified lawyers or judges. However, a Stoic mechanic is expected to obtain the necessary wisdom that enables them to fix cars and to treat people justly at the same time, as this will have an impact on their own well-being and the well-being of others.

---

* Stoicism names a few exceptions to this. The biggest is young children, who are considered unable to think and act rationally.

Panaetius understood that one of his roles in life was to be a Greek Stoic philosopher charged with mentoring statesmen and generals of the Roman Republic. He did not believe that everyone is (or necessarily should be) born equal when it comes to wealth, health, and the various other things Stoics consider to be external to human happiness. He had no issue with being powerful or wealthy. He understood that the elite would never grant an audience to a poor man. He knew that it was precisely his power, wealth, and social accolades that gave him access and authority. So Panaetius leveraged them to get closer to the ears and minds of those in Roman command. Once he had obtained a seat at the table, he reminded the powerful (and himself) that most building blocks are placed by others, including those with whom we share no familial ties. If his companions thought otherwise, he called them out on it. He chose his words carefully, striking at the very heart of their social role and the self-made myth. He tried to make sure that everyone in his circle understood that no one, whether a general in war or a leading statesman at home, could have accomplished deeds of great service without the support of his fellow men and women.

Panaetius was intent on prodding his finger into the Roman elite's proud chests and social bubbles because he did not want them to take others for granted or become complacent in their duties to Rome and her people. He wanted them to check their privileges. He wanted them to remember that the greatness of their beloved Republic, and their social standing within it, was only made possible via tremendous group effort. He was adamant that there was no such thing as the self-made man and implied that believing otherwise was to believe in a mythical creature. Speaking truth to power did not diminish Panaetius' influence but amplified it. Long after his death, his words would inspire generations of Roman elite, all the way up to Emperor Marcus Aurelius — the most famous and powerful Stoic of all time.

⌐⌐⌐⌐

In some respects, the venture capitalist Nick Hanauer is a modern-day version of Panaetius. While the latter's family enjoyed prestige and local celebrity in Rhodes, Nick comes from a renowned Seattle family who have owned and held shares in various major businesses located in the city. His early success came from the fact that he and his brother, Adrian, were heirs to the Pacific Coast Feather Company, which has been headquartered in Seattle for over a hundred years. Nick built on this financial foundation by persuading Amazon's founder and CEO Jeff Bezos to relocate to Seattle and by becoming the first investor outside of Bezos' family to buy up Amazon stock options. By the time Nick sold his shares, in 2000, he was well on his way to becoming an exceedingly wealthy and shrewd investor. More success followed when he sold the marketing firm he had cofounded to Microsoft, another Seattle-based company, for $6.3 billion. This transaction added $270 million to his personal fortune and shot him up the rankings of America's most powerful people.

By this time, the Hanauer brothers were garnering money as if it grew on trees. They were riding wave after wave of popular media coverage, particularly in their local newspaper, the *Seattle Times*. Clearly, they were the men of the moment. Adrian had won the heart of soccer fans all over the city when he used his money and contacts to ensure that his soccer club (which became known as the Seattle Sounders) was awarded Major League Soccer status.[5] Nick had proven that he had what it took to win in the zero-sum game called venture capitalism. Both could afford to buy private jets, penthouses, yachts, and multiple sports teams with the same ease that the middle class buy secondhand cars and first homes.[6] Yet by the mid-2000s, Nick began to wonder what really mattered to him. Who did he want to be and what did he stand for?

As Nick answered these questions for himself, it quickly became apparent that while he and his brother had worked hard and made some smart choices along the way, they weren't deserving of everything they had achieved. For one thing, both had certainly received more than their fair share of luck. Reflecting on this, Nick began to doubt the validity of the self-made myth and quickly concluded that no one, no matter how successful, deserved to earn a thousand times the median wage. Further, he recognized that most, if not all, people in the rarified 1 percent of society were gaming the system to their advantage.

Nick also spotted the vested interest the extremely wealthy had in upholding two additional myths: (1) trickle-down economics, which maintains that what is good for the wealthy is good for the masses, who will eventually benefit from the spoils of the elite; and (2) that people are naturally selfish maximizers who only look out for their best interests, and anyone who does not deserves to be shafted because such behavior is "irrational." This distortion of the concept of rationality was alien to Nick because of what he had been taught in his philosophy classes at the University of Washington.[7] While the philosophical greats he read as a student — including Socrates, Plato, Aristotle, the Stoics, and Immanuel Kant — all emphasized the value of rationality, none associated it with selfishness or used it to support wealth accumulation and concentration. None of them said that humans operate as island states, completely independent of one another. On the contrary, these great thinkers talked about rationality explicitly in terms of selflessness, reciprocity, community, and kinship.

Just like Panaetius, Nick wanted to call out the lie of the "self-made man" in such a way that people had little choice but to sit up and listen. Also, like Panaetius, Nick had no issue with being powerful or wealthy because he understood that remarkably few people will listen to a poor man. Nick understood that it was precisely his power, riches, and social accolades that gave him the access and authority to speak out against his fellow plutocrats and remind them, and their supporters, that what is good for the people is good for them. To think otherwise is backward. In an effort to maintain their myths, many of the rich businesspeople Nick rubbed shoulders with had failed to recognize that the functionality of their beloved capitalism and the fruits they earned from it were harvested by the workers they were belying.

In 2010, Nick posed himself an altogether more difficult question: What would he do about it? How exactly would he use his role as a plutocrat to shed light on the issue and bring about change? How would he refute those who said he was a liar, hypocrite, or traitor? Many of his opponents argued that Nick should just give his money away if he felt that bad about being rich! However, when he looked at the bigger picture of income equality and the prevalence of the three myths, he knew that simply giving away money, paying more taxes, or offering a higher salary to his employees was not a very effective strategy for bringing about social change. Nick did not want to pay more taxes or higher salaries. He wanted *everyone* in his tax bracket to pay more taxes and offer a living wage to their workers because in a world that values justice that is the right thing to do.

Armed with this vision and purpose, Nick took the fight to a system that openly celebrates the fact that, since 1980, the wealthiest Americans have nearly tripled their share of national income while the poorest 50 percent have lost about a third of their share.[8] Thinking carefully about his social roles, his communal obligations, and the sharp skill set that he had honed during his dog-eat-dog days as a venture capitalist, Nick brought his business acumen and tenacity to the table. He poured his time, money, and social network into building a strong team that had both the skill set and the mindset for progressive policies and lobbying. He reasoned that if a business thrived once you secured funding and leadership, the same would hold true for a public cause. The cause he chose was, at the time, groundbreaking. He wanted to increase Seattle's minimum wage so that all employers in his home city would pay a fifteen-dollar living wage — even the restaurant owners who had always managed to shift the wage bill to the American customer in the form of tips. He was adamant that employers be held accountable, no matter how much they objected or threatened to leave or boycott the city.

Nick knew it would be a rocky road full of angry opposition, but he was undeterred. It was a case of "go big or go home." His fellow plutocrats panicked, but he pushed. *Forbes* magazine called him "near insane"; he shrugged.[9] They felt threatened, but he refused to back down. Instead, he refocused, doubled down on his efforts, and remained confident that the right economic stimulus would carry the poor out of the downward spiral of food stamps and government top-ups. Nick just had to do his part in calibrating the mechanisms and oiling the capitalist machinery. For inspiration, he looked to Henry Ford,* who a hundred years previously had shocked and amazed American industry heads and newspaper editors by offering his workers an opportunity to join his shared profit plan. Under Ford's plan, his employees effectively doubled their daily pay as long as they met company stipulations, which included regularly contributing to a personal savings account.

Ford reasoned that higher wages would lead to increased worker retention and that this would reduce the costs associated with new hires (turnover rate was 370 percent), lateness, and absenteeism.[10] His decision generated positive headlines that placed the Ford Motor Company in the media spotlight, a ripple effect that attracted not only new workers but customers, too. Workers who

---

* Henry Ford is an American hero for the ways he revolutionized industry and treated his workers, among other things, but as we note in chapter 2, no one is perfect. In this case, Ford's well-known Nazi sympathies were appalling and should also be remembered. Stoics should praise someone's admirable actions without excusing, or failing to learn from, their vicious ones.

were encouraged to save up for their own car provided one of the best forms of advertising. If they did not have money problems, they were happier and more productive versions of themselves. By sharing in the profits, they were also more willing to shoulder any problems and fix them. Ford's new wage policy improved his workers' conditions and had a huge impact on company profits, the automobile sector, and blue-collar jobs in America generally — again proving that no person or company is an island. Other car manufacturers, anxious to keep up with Ford's soaring profits and recognition as one of the nation's great companies, followed Henry Ford's lead and paid their own workers a living wage. The dominoes tumbled and other sectors, who were afraid to lose workers to the automobile industry, in turn, increased wages. It is no exaggeration to say that one man's vision brought millions of American families into the middle class and helped kick-start the consumerism (for good and for bad) that formed the cornerstone of American life, politics, and economics over the next fifty years.

Nick did not have to wait long to see a Henry Ford–like ripple effect for the minimum-wage policy he was championing. Passed in June 2014, the new law mandated that, by 2018, all big businesses (those with five hundred employees or more) located in Seattle would raise the minimum hourly wage from $9.47 to $15.00.* The first victory was a resounding one. By and large, restaurant owners did not follow through with their threats to leave the city or boycott. As long as businesses stayed afloat, people were not fired or made redundant. New restaurants and bars opened at a

---

* In 2019, the federal minimum hourly wage was $7.25. If the federal minimum wage had been doubled to $15, it would have immediately addressed the decline in fortunes of the middle class and the fact that the federal minimum wage has not increased in line with inflation since 1968. Paying people properly is a question of justice and therefore something that a Stoic is very concerned about. No one can be indifferent to the difficulties faced by workers, especially as inequality magnifies with each passing year.

higher rate than businesses failed, and the number of jobs in the sector grew from 134,000 to 157,000.[11] Such figures should not come as a surprise, since waitstaff and their families could now afford to eat out and spend extra money on things they had long gone without. Extra cash in people's pockets went on to stimulate other sectors and increase the disposable income that these workers themselves had — some of which fed back into restaurants, in what can only be described as a virtuous circle. There were numerous other benefits, too. Job turnover rates were reduced by 8 percent, which lowered hiring and training costs, and undoubtedly improved customer-service quality. Higher wages meant that the most experienced full-time workers were valued more than their inexperienced counterparts, as their additional skills and training, all too often ignored or undermined, were now seen as assets that deserved to be remunerated at a fifteen-dollar hourly wage. This meant that experienced staff members were no longer in the precarious and unreasonable position of being stuck in a "dead-end" job. Even the part-time inexperienced workers who got their hours cut following Seattle's mandatory wage increase did not see a notable reduction in salary. While they were unable to capitalize fully on the wage increase, their ability to save remained the same and their reduced working hours meant they could more easily pursue education, training programs, and other initiatives that would allow them to bypass the low-wage labor market entirely.[12]

Further evidence showed the premises for rejecting Seattle's minimum-wage increase were false, and the battle cries denouncing it were at best hot air and at worst scaremongering. For all the proclamations of "insanity" leveled on Nick and his fellow visionaries, any detrimental impact on the marginal costs for large business was negligible. There was no clear indication of price increases on products manufactured in Seattle, and food prices did not shoot up to compensate for increases in supermarket wages (however, the childcare sector has struggled and probably needs state-level support to adjust).[13] While new businesses found it difficult to accommodate the increase in the minimum wage, as they were unable to take advantage of the considerable reductions in the staff turnover rate, the average employer faced only minor disruptions to their business operations over the transition period.[14]

Nick's intuition had been right. Not only could Seattle sustain a fifteen-dollar hourly wage but its people and businesses, who were not islands but highly connected nodes, could prosper. With hard and independently verified evidence, Nick and his team had slain the rhetoric of naysayers. They had burst the self-made myth by doing more than criticizing it. Using Nick's money and power, they had debunked it by envisioning and supporting a re-emergence of the middle class — the group of people responsible for the health of an economy.

For Dan Price, the Seattle-based CEO of Gravity Payments, taking care of people doesn't come down to money but a sense of fairness and moral integrity. It is simply a decision he chose to make. Against conventional wisdom, at just twenty-three years old, he made the decision to weather the 2008 financial crisis without laying people off because he believed that a leader should fight the storm with his staff instead of casting them aside to save his company. Then, in 2015, Price felt he could, and should, do more for those who had got him onto the cover of *Entrepreneur* magazine.[15] So he took the unusual step of cutting his $1.1-million salary so that everyone who worked for him could have a raise. Price wasn't playing around. The plan was, and still is, for everyone at his company to earn at least $70,000 by 2024, including the janitors and cleaners.[16] One quarter of his workforce doubled their salary overnight.[17] His reason for doing it? He believed that as the CEO, his role was to support his employees' emotional well-being and that he had a moral imperative to buck the income inequality trend, at least within the four walls of his own company. After all, a country's living conditions are considered favorable when the average citizen is better off, that is, when they have access to good public health care, good public education, and a salary that allows them to comfortably meet their rent payments or save up for their own home.

Some media outlets championed Price's move, but others openly mocked him and hoped for his company's demise for no other reason than they wanted him (and his employees) to fail. Many in such quarters labeled Price a "socialist." Even talk-show host Trevor Noah did so in a tongue-in-cheek attempt to show how pervasive the misuse of the term *socialism* has become in America.[18] When used in a derogatory fashion to derail anyone who attempts to use capitalist mechanisms to share the fruits of its spoils, the term really is nothing more than a thinly veiled threat leveled by those who are frightened of losing power and privilege in the game they have rigged. Make no mistake, that is not capitalism. That is bullying. And as for doing the right thing for the right reason, that's not socialism. That's Stoicism! That's why it is profoundly Stoic to point out the fact that there are plenty of plutocrats who have done nothing to improve things, precisely because in their cowardice, injustice, greed, or ignorance they have chosen to hide behind the false narratives that justify their wealth and position.

If you are not in a position of power, it is difficult to know how best to respond to unjust economic inequality and the increased gulf between the rich and the poor. A lot of people, even those who practice Stoicism, can be a little too quick to shrug their shoulders and ask themselves (or their friends on social media), "What has this to do with me?" Frankly, a more interesting and an altogether more Stoic question is to ask, "Based on my four roles and the degrees of freedom given to me, what can I do to improve things?" When answering this question, and as Panaetius suggested, we should consider our own individual nature, our personal circumstances, our career choices or job, and our knowledge or expertise. We must also ask ourselves, "Does my decision reflect what a virtuous person would do in my position?"

Of course, when it comes to addressing unjust income inequality in society, some people have more direct ways to help than others. Like Dan Price and Nick Hanauer, if someone earns a millionaire's salary and has the ability to influence others in business and government, they could share their salary and their company's earnings with everyone in their workforce. They could equally choose to lobby companies and politicians to change industry practices and laws for the betterment of the lower and middle classes and the environment. What about you, particularly if you don't earn a high salary, or even any salary at all? You can review your four roles and take action in whatever ways are appropriate and effective given your circumstances and preferences. For instance, simply voicing an opinion can be effective and powerful; say, by questioning the assumptions and arguments of a relative who believes some workers don't have a right to a living wage. All citizens can use their vote and their voice to challenge policies that champion tax breaks for the wealthy. Simply reflecting upon one's own privileges can also be valuable. Ask yourself: How much of your success has depended upon the help of others? Finally, we all have the ability to cheer on those who do the right thing for the right reason. This shows them that they are not alone and that other people value their efforts. It is a mistake to think that our heroes don't need our encouragement or a helping hand. They got to where they are because people like us believed in their message, felt inspired by it, and shared it with others.

Further, it is a mistake to imagine our heroes as somehow distinct from other people or even from ourselves. Everyone possesses the ability to question what they are told about the way the world can, and should, work. Anyone, from any walk of life, can foster the courage and conviction to do things differently. We all can be true visionaries armed with a deep understanding of the fact that we can only succeed when our self-interest begins, aligns, and ends with the interests of the world community. Each one of us might become a hero for someone else. In our own way, we can encourage people to come together, share a vision, and work toward the goal of improving our collective circumstances, lifting everyone up in solidarity and reciprocity. Helping others and recognizing that others also help us is the best way to put to rest the self-made myth.

The ancient Stoics taught that a rational human does not enjoy being isolated and alone. If in doubt, you only need look to the world of sports. Sports fans are known to have an impact on the game. In American football, fans are encouraged to make noise when their team is defending because it makes it harder for the visiting team's quarterback to clearly communicate his intentions to the rest of the offense. In soccer, the crowd gets on its feet and cheers for their goalkeeper when they are faced with a penalty shoot-out. The positive impact of home support on team performance is so great that it led the Seattle Seahawks to retire the number 12 jersey in honor of their fans (on an eleven-player football team, fans are considered the "twelfth player"). However, we all know that one fan does not make that much noise and thus has no power to influence the outcome. If any individual supporter decided to stay at home, players wouldn't notice. But imagine if all the home fans decided not to attend because they didn't feel that their presence would make a difference. What would happen then? Certainly, the home team's performance would suffer and they might be more likely to lose.* When you buy a ticket to a game, you do so in the belief that, along with all the others joining you in the stands, your collective presence will help your team

---

* During the Covid-19 pandemic, many sport teams and commentators noticed that the home-field advantage disappeared and, in some cases, affected the end result.

win. You do this even though stadium attendance or how your team plays is, for the most part, outside of your control. Whether in the blistering sun, the pouring rain, or the freezing snow, you go to the game anyway because that is what makes you a good fan. You do it because, deep down, you know that Panaetius is right — no one is an island!

PANAETIUS' QUESTIONS

Being a member of the Scipionic Circle certainly had its advantages when it came to influencing Roman thought. Panaetius and many other influential Stoics owed their success to a lot of people: rich and poor, citizen and slave. It is important to remember that no one, no matter how successful, can operate in isolation.

- Think carefully about how success and financial wealth is built using other people's effort, time, skills, social leverage, and perhaps fortune or misfortune. How does this change your view of those who have achieved more than you? How does it make you think about those who are less fortunate than yourself?

Remember that everyone has four roles. The first and primary role is the simple fact of being a rational human being. The second is shaped by your individual nature: your likes, dislikes, personality traits, and odd quirks. The third is embodied by your personal circumstances. The fourth relates to the path you wish to take in life.

- Given your four roles, how would you combine them to most effectively journey toward *eudaimonia*?

CHAPTER 6

PUT PEOPLE IN CIRCLES, NOT BOXES

A man separates himself from his neighbor by his own hatred
or rejection, not realizing that he has thereby severed himself
from the wider society of fellow citizens.
— Marcus Aurelius, *Meditations* 11.8

Personal relationships were very important to Marcus Aurelius. So important, in fact, that for the first entry of his diary (which we now refer to as *Meditations*), he paid homage to the people that helped mold him into a good man, a competent soldier, and a powerful philosopher-emperor. In the most challenging moments of his reign, most of which he spent camped in the harsh frozen German wilderness, Marcus no doubt found comfort in returning to that page of gratitude, which acknowledged that he was far from being self-made.

Some Roman emperors would have basked in the glory of their many titles. However, Marcus knew that an inflated ego would only hinder him. He might have been the most powerful citizen in Rome, but he was not her only citizen and Rome wasn't the only empire. Consequently, being a good emperor was not just about fulfilling specific duties and obligations toward his own citizens, but also about understanding that he was a member of a larger community of world citizens. Under the watchful eye of the Roman Senate, Rome's citizens, and her enemies, Marcus leaned on Stoicism to remain levelheaded, immune to flattery, and critical of mere opinion — both his own and that of others. His problems, meanwhile, were tackled by taking a cosmic view of the world, which allowed him to see things in a more objective light. This Stoic practice of visualization served to remind him that his life wasn't the be-all and end-all, but instead just one of the many that coexisted on Earth. The "view from above" also helped Marcus to guard himself against the false impressions,* snap judgments, and superficial frivolities[1] that proliferate when we allow others to cater to our self-indulged existence.

Stoic philosophy complemented Marcus' serious and scholarly temperament, strong sense of duty, and introspective manner, all of which kept his feet firmly on the ground. From an early age, his Stoic teachers conveyed to him the importance of training the mind's eye, which should not covet gold, glory, power, or sexual prowess but instead a desire to be of good and truthful character.[2] Despite the various temptations surrounding Marcus, and the excuses people would have been willing to make on his behalf, he went to great lengths not to abuse his authority — a feat he achieved by not acting upon his lust for his female slaves, by not condemning others in a fit of anger, and by not neglecting any of his roles as a husband, father, friend, soldier, and political leader. Marcus was also careful not to take sides. He was mindful of poking his nose into matters that did not concern him and chose instead to focus on identifying where he fell short of virtuous living.[3] This is something that all Stoics should strive for.

---

*   For Stoics, moral responsibility consists in making appropriate judgments about impressions and thoughts. When confronted with any impression, a Stoic must decide to accept that impression as something that corresponds to reality or, alternatively, decide that it does not correspond to reality. If they are not sure, they are instructed to withhold assent. Consider Epictetus' poignant dictum in *Enchiridion* 5: "People are not disturbed by events, but by the view they take about events."

It is true that Marcus lived in an insulated bubble of wealth, power, and comfort, one created for him by the emperors Hadrian and Antoninus Pius, who also happened to be his adoptive father. In the absence of poverty, it might seem easy for Marcus to focus on virtuous living. There is no doubt that he was privileged. But how many people use their privilege virtuously? How many privileged individuals actively use their position and power to improve the lives of those less fortunate than themselves? At the same time, the Stoics have always upheld that neither poverty nor any other socioeconomic or physical characteristic prevents us from experiencing *eudaimonia*. Our present circumstances or social position never exclude us from doing the right thing for the right reason — on the contrary, they are the means by which we choose to do what is right (or what is wrong). That's not to say that it isn't extremely difficult to think about our duties toward others (particularly beyond our immediate family) when we are dodging bullets, attempting to hold down three jobs, or chronically ill in bed. However, *eudaimonia* becomes impossible to reach when we firmly believe that we are deserving of success just because we happen to be born into a certain family and come from a particular country, or because we have never taken a long hard look at ourselves. Vice and virtue can rise during easier and simpler times as much as during times of hardship and uncertainty. No one is immune from vice. No one is excluded from virtue.

Roman imperial life had both its privileges and its burdens, and Marcus Aurelius sought to take advantage of all his opportunities so that he could best carry the load. The same could not be said for his younger brother, Lucius Verus, who despite also having Antoninus as an adopted father, and having received the same Stoic education, failed to do much with the prospects his position afforded him. While Marcus sought wisdom by learning all he could from Antoninus and his Stoic teachers in order to become an excellent emperor himself, Lucius sought the hedonistic thrills of the chariot races, gladiatorial fights, theater performances, tavern brawls, and gambling.[4] Clearly, being insulated in a bubble of wealth and power is no guarantee of virtuous behavior nor indicative of a person's desire to achieve *eudaimonia*.

Upon Antoninus' death, and much to the surprise of Rome, Marcus insisted his reign be a joint one between him and his brother, whereby Lucius, who certainly had some leadership qualities, ruled everyone except Marcus, who held ultimate authority. Marcus was dedicated to the welfare of his brother and saw this act as a way of strengthening their bond. It was also a strong signal to the elite in the Empire that Lucius was very much invited into Marcus' circles of concern and not someone he would simply toss aside because he possessed some inconvenient flaws.

The idea of visualizing our relationships with one another as a set of concentric circles is a very Stoic one. Based on the teachings of Zeno of Citium and Panaetius (see chapters 1 and 5, respectively), these circles were formally depicted by Marcus' and Lucius' contemporary Hierocles, who was by all accounts a "grave and holy man."[5] Hierocles held that a Stoic's relationship with others starts with the circle of the "self" and thereupon expands into a successive set that encompasses family, friends, community, and all humanity. Hierocles stressed the idea that we should aim to draw the circles of concern inward, thus bringing the whole of humanity closer to our sense of self until we are able to recognize ourselves in all of humanity and all of humanity in ourselves. This does not mean to say that Stoics believe that we should treat everyone in exactly the same way, as if all people formed some homogenous group with identical behaviors, interests, and expectations. For one thing, it would be inappropriate (and unwise) to have, or to hope for, the same level of connection with close members of our family as we do with work colleagues or strangers in the street. For another, being fair to people is, among other things, to acknowledge both our commonalities and our differences and to behave with that in mind. It is also about treating people as fellow world inhabitants and giving them their due, as our social position and relationship dictates.

One particularly poignant way of considering our roles and the different concentric circles that surround us is to recognize that, while we have duties toward our fellow citizens, the geographic national borders that distinguish one country from another are, at least in some sense, arbitrary and imaginary. Of course, different countries have different cultures and governments, but as Hierocles might say, a good person understands that everyone, no matter where and how they live, is part of the world community.* In fact, as we contract our circles of concern inward — for example, by treating cousins like siblings, and fellow citizens like cousins, and so on — we would, in many respects, be inclined to treat recent immigrants and foreign visitors as fellow nationals![6] This Stoic practice thus provides a sharp contrast to the placing of people we don't know in boxes, a quick sorting method that all too often categorizes rather than humanizes people.

The circles of concern express two Stoic convictions. First, that humans naturally feel a more direct or pressing connection with some people (such as family and friends) than they do with others. Second, that all human beings belong to a single world community (a state that the ancient Greeks referred to as a *cosmopolis*) and therefore should be able to participate as world citizens, regardless of their gender, ethnicity, sexuality, country of origin, or bank balance. Marcus alludes to this cosmopolitan ideal when he writes that "a man separates himself from his neighbor by his own hatred or rejection, not realizing that he has thereby severed himself from the wider society of fellow citizens." His choice of words reflects what he learned as a battle-hardened

---

* His exact terminology might have been different, as it is more likely that he would have referred to the global community as "the great cosmic city."

general who, despite being dragged from war campaign to war campaign, didn't enjoy the glory of defending the corners of his empire nor his claim to the Roman seat of power.

The first challenge to Marcus' throne came as early as the first year of his reign when, in 161 CE, Vologases IV of Parthia and his army easily dispatched battle-shy Roman soldiers stationed in Armenia. Sensing the advantage, Vologases battled on and goaded Rome to roar into action, as he set about taking Syria. Although Marcus was far from a warmonger, he would not be bullied or beaten. His empire would be no paper tiger. So, he countered the emerging threat by sending along his most capable officers and generals and repositioning three legions that had been stationed near the Rhine and Danube. The plan worked; the Romans won comfortably, and Marcus regained control. Unfortunately, this inadvertently triggered a chain of events that meant that, from then on, Marcus was destined to spend the majority of the rest of his life in the no-man's-land between the Empire and the warring settlements of various Germanic tribes, who were not afraid to raid and wreak havoc on Marcus' citizens.

Given the cards he was dealt, it was to Marcus' great credit that he did not fall victim to complacency. This is what many expected of him, since under the guidance of Antoninus, he had never once stepped out of the safe and comfortable confines of Italy. It also speaks of his remarkable character that he didn't lord his position or use it to divide those who ruled from those who were ruled over. On the contrary, Marcus used his authority to break down the proverbial boxes people were placed in and encouraged a different take on humanity — one understood through the Stoic lens of Hierocles' circles of concern. As often as possible, Marcus freed slaves, appointed guardians for the orphaned, improved social conditions for the poor, and ensured that the streets of Rome were clean and in good working condition. This was no mean feat, given that, aside from perennial war,

Marcus' reign began with a major flood that swept away livestock, destroyed buildings, and led to food shortages, hunger, and disease. However, in his dealings with enemies, even more so than with his subjects, Marcus both excelled as a leader and showed his truest cosmopolitan colors as a Stoic philosopher. Conscious of his role as the protector of Rome's citizens and political interests, Marcus took the long-term view that brokering peace treaties, integrating and resettling suitable tribes into the empty borders of the Empire (which had been especially hard hit by the Antonine plague[7]), and rewarding good behavior was a much more rational and productive way of dealing with Germanic insurgents. He did not take pride in capturing even the most hostile among them. In fact, he wrote critically of those who enjoyed enslaving the fierce nomadic Sarmatian Iazyges (see *Meditations* 10.10).

On various occasions, Marcus lifted the restrictions he had imposed on the Germanic tribes only to be repaid with backstabbing and heartache.[8] But he almost always resisted paying them back in kind. Even the Iazyges, whom Marcus deemed fit for extermination after they had crossed him one too many times, were spared after he caught wind of General Avidius Cassius' mutiny thousands of miles away in modern-day Turkey. Convinced of the immediate need to quell this rogue uprising, Marcus offered the tribe a peace settlement, as long as they agreed to supply eight thousand warriors, release a hundred thousand Roman prisoners of war, and help him to neutralize any threats emerging from their heartlands. The Iazyges, exceptionally grateful for Marcus' change of heart, proved, this time, to be people of their word and excellent allies. They helped Marcus to divide, conquer, and trap the other Germanic tribes, who, far from being annihilated, were forced to settle in the Empire and pay taxes in exchange for eventual citizenship.[9]

Marcus was a rare Roman emperor in that his treatment toward those who conspired against him demonstrated that he considered their humanity first and their betrayal second. He would have pardoned the traitorous Avidius Cassius if the Senate hadn't first decided to make him an enemy of the state. On receiving Cassius' severed head, a gift he never asked for, Marcus ordered that what remained of him be buried with full military honors. As for the Syrian city of Antioch (located in modern-day Turkey) that had provided a platform for Cassius' rebellion, Marcus did not punish its citizens by razing it to the ground — far from it! Instead, he banned the city from holding public sporting events. That's right. For their part in the coup, people would not be allowed to organize or watch official gladiatorial battles or chariot races![10] Such a declaration hardly seems unreasonable, even by modern standards. Indeed, it shows that Marcus saw war and acts of treason as opportunities to practice virtue and live up to the Stoic cosmopolitan ideal of extending his circles of concern to cover even those who had wronged him.

When it comes to evaluating a person's choices, Marcus would assert, as would any of the other ancient Stoics,* that no matter where people are from, we should treat them with the due care and consideration that less-cosmopolitan thinkers might only afford to their closest friends and family members. Epictetus' lessons were passed on to Marcus by his philosophical tutor, Rusticus, who ensured that the young emperor in the making understood that judging someone based on their nationality was foolishness (*Discourses* 1.9):

> Where one is asked where one is from, never reply "I'm Athenian" or "I'm Corinthian," but rather "I'm a citizen of the universe." For why say, in fact, that you're Athenian

---

* The Roman Stoic Seneca, for instance, states (*On Leisure* 4.1): "Let us embrace two states in our minds — one great and truly shared in which gods and men are held together, in which we do not look to this or that corner, but measure the boundaries of our state with the sun; the other into which the circumstance of our birth enrolls us."

rather than just a citizen of that corner in which your poor body was thrown down at the time of your birth?*

Place of birth has never been a factor in judging someone's moral worth in Stoicism. The Stoic founder Zeno and his two successors, Cleanthes and Chrysippus, were all immigrants. Both Zeno and Cleanthes were penniless on their arrival into Athens. Birthplace was not an issue for the Roman Stoics, either, and as Marcus showed in his treatment toward hostile Germanic tribes, it certainly was not an impediment to Roman citizenship. In fact, as with early American history, the stories and achievements of immigrants were woven into the very fabric of the Roman Republic (and later the Empire[11]).

This issue of birthplace, citizenship, and whether to embrace or turn away immigrants speaks to us today, of course. While there may be legitimate concerns about the intentions behind a guest's reasons for wanting to be in a country, or their willingness to follow the house rules, the overwhelming majority of immigrants (and tourists, for that matter), just like the great majority of nationals, don't want to destroy the good will or social contract that a country offers. Most people wishing to relocate to a new country just want to actively participate in society as best they can. As authors, Leo and I are speaking here of "people" in general, but we are also speaking for ourselves. Leo is an American of Greek Argentine origin, and I am a Brit who continues to live and work in more than my fair share of countries, from China to Colombia! As two immigrants, we want to offer the best of our skills and abilities to the countries that we have chosen to call home. We want to make the best of the opportunities that have

---

* These sentiments are not dissimilar to those of the Christian apostle Paul when he wrote in Galatians 3:28: "There is neither Jew nor Greek, there is neither bond nor free, there is neither male nor female."

been presented to us, whether that be in the army, in a classroom, or out and about in our communities. We want to show gratitude to those who have embraced us, even though we were not born in the same corner of Earth.

ᚱᚱᚱᚱᚱ

In 1994, Hamdi Ulukaya left Turkey for the United States with one simple aim. He would go to university to learn English, in the hope that it would help him to integrate quickly into the country that had offered him a chance to escape the tumultuous politics of his homeland. Given his desire to embrace American culture, Ulukaya never envisioned that his Kurdish heritage would play such a prominent role in his billionaire journey as the CEO of Chobani, the Greek yogurt company. When he first landed on American soil, he didn't know much about yogurt. What he did understand, though, having grown up in a shepherding family, was the importance of good strong leadership, which goes both ways: Sheep are lost without someone to guide them, and a shepherd is nothing if not for their sheep.

Up in the remote mountains, where Ulukaya spent his formative years, money buys you nothing. The key to success is the well-being of your flock and your ability to survive harsh unpredictable conditions. This, in turn, requires that you watch out for wolves and keep them at bay, while also identifying which of the sheep are likely to stray and which ones are sick. When your survival is threatened by the wanderings of just one member of the flock, the presence of just one predator, or the passing of one bad storm, you quickly learn to trust your instincts and cultivate an unspoken agreement that "we are all in this together" because "what is good for you is good for me." For Ulukaya, this understanding of how the world works led to his rather alternative vision of the CEO playbook.

In his early days as a yogurt-factory owner, Ulukaya was

sure of only one thing. More than anything else, he had to instill a sense of belief into his factory workers, who had been told
by their previous employer that they were of little value and that
their jobs did not matter. He started with a team-building exercise
that involved taking paintbrushes to the dilapidated factory walls.
It soon became five years of rebuilding and rebranding, which
gave the staff a new lease on life. Together, they worked nights,
long days, and holidays. It more than paid off: In 2007, the tiny
operation served only one local grocer, but by 2012, it had become a behemoth fed by $1 billion of annual sales.[12] However,
Ulukaya and his team did not want to stop there. They wanted to
change the way people thought about business etiquette.

For Ulukaya, it was strange that so many CEO playbooks
ruled that employees — the very people responsible for the company's success — were to be made redundant so that the shareholders who invested money, but not effort, time, sweat, or tears,
could see a significant return on investment. Why was there no
return on investment for those who were giving everything except money? Why didn't their value go up in line with corpo-
rate profit? Why weren't companies and shareholders concerned
about their needs?

Ulukaya wanted to demonstrate to the business world that the
most successful companies were those who took care of their employees by rewarding their loyalty and hard work. He wanted to
show other CEOs and their shareholders that offering a helping
hand to those who need it brings goodwill, profits, prizes, brand
recognition, and a strong market share — all of which a company
needs to flourish in the full sense of the word. The first step in
Ulukaya's action plan was to give his full-time workers 10 percent of his company shares.[13] His second step was to give those
employees with newborn children six weeks of full paid parental

leave.* Convinced that Chobani could do more for the community and that he could shepherd a larger flock, Ulukaya then opened his circles of concern to include refugees and economic migrants — two groups of people who, just like everybody else, contribute far more positively to society once they can put down roots and integrate. Given his role as a CEO, Ulukaya felt the best way he could make this happen was to give legal immigrants jobs at his factory. Many reasons were put forward to stop this third step from materializing. As part of a media smear campaign, Ulukaya was told, "Immigrants don't speak English." He said, "Let's get translators." He was told, "They don't have transportation." He said, "Let's get buses."[14] So he did. Then he threw out the notion that immigrants were a cheap form of labor and paid those who did the same job and had the same level of experience the same salary, regardless of birthplace. This instilled a sense of pride, belonging, and agency throughout his workforce. It also ensured that the factory wage was not undercut or undermined. No one was put in a box labeled "immigrant" or "disposable." Instead, everyone was protected within Ulukaya's circles of concern, which were underpinned by his view that there are only two kinds of people in this world — those who work for Chobani and those who do not.

Both Hamdi Ulukaya and Marcus Aurelius, albeit in vastly different jobs and different times, demonstrate how embodying the Stoic principle of "putting people in circles, not boxes" can lead to personal success and improve everyone's welfare. Both were committed to acting this way despite opposition to their ideals. Unfortunately, such opposition is not surprising. There are many conflicting loyalties and tensions that can, and do, occur when we try to prioritize our various duties and obligations toward family,

---

* In contrast to most EU countries, which legally support paid maternal and paternal leave, the majority of US states have no legal stipulation that requires paid maternal or paternal leave.

friends, colleagues, and the wider world. Most of our home, business, and social life involves interactions with other people, some of whom we like, some of whom we don't; some of whom we are related to and friends with, and most of whom we are not. Within all these relationships, we can promote (or weaken) Stoic values and thus create (or endanger) the possibility of a more harmonious family life, workplace, and society generally. The idea of putting people in circles need not take on the utilitarian notion of the greatest good for the greatest number. Rather, it should reflect the Stoic thought that if someone acts in the interests of the whole of humanity — not just most of society, and not just for one's family, tribe, or community — then, and only then, might that action benefit all individuals as part of the whole.

MARCUS' QUESTIONS

Marcus Aurelius spent a lot of time at war and had to deal with a lot of people he didn't like. Some of them were supposed to be his friends — or at least on his side. Others were considered the enemy because they fought under an opposing banner. In his personal diary, Marcus reflected on their humanity and on their reasons for battle. He pondered the cosmopolitan nature of the universe that connects us all. The "view from above" kept him humble and cautious about the kinds of orders he gave his legions and generals.

- Imagine someone you consider to be your enemy. What is it about them that you are opposed to or despise? Would you see them differently if you discovered that you were related to them?

CHAPTER 7

ONLY THE EDUCATED
ARE FREE

The finest and most fitting fruits for those who have received
a true philosophical education are peace of mind, fearlessness,
and freedom.... Thus, none but the educated can be free.
— Epictetus, *Discourses* 2.1.21–23

Every ancient Stoic, stretching right the way back to the
founder, Zeno, believed that every prototypical adult had,
in accordance with their social role, a duty to instruct those who
sought wisdom. Such teaching was not restricted to a formalized
school setting, and it did not involve a higher education certificate. Nor was it limited to a specific curriculum that would enable
you to pass a national test, obtain a high-paying job, or merely
win an argument. Learning was instead centered on the "art of
living," a lifelong subject matter that involved the continual craft-
ing and reworking of the self.[1] In practice, this involved becoming
more intentional about when and how you spoke, or remained
silent, and when and how you acted or withdrew.

Stoic teachers, including Epictetus, practiced the "art of living" just as much as they taught it. They sought to equip their
students, and themselves, with the necessary tools for the ac-
quisition of knowledge; traditional training consisted of logic,
physics, rhetoric, and ethics. Over time, such learning revealed
the inner beauty of a steadily transformed soul. The state of the

latter was made apparent not only in how an individual expressed themselves in their personal pursuits (some of which might fall under what we now call self-development), but also in how they fulfilled their civic duties and upheld their status as a good citizen.[2]

Clearly, Epictetus' statement that "None but the educated can be free" goes beyond the kind of scholarly knowledge that university professors share and, perhaps, indulge in. By way of analogy, we can see that Epictetus is, in fact, instructing us to craft our mind and body like a carpenter who works their wood by successively cutting, sanding, and polishing it with wax until it fulfills its intended purpose. That said, it was not Epictetus but Sphaerus, a pragmatic student of both Zeno and Cleanthes, who sketched out the design for how Stoics should approach education and philosophy as a way of life.

Sphaerus was originally from Borysthenes, also known as Olbia, a Hellenic harbor city located in modern-day Ukraine,* just off the mouth of the Dnieper River and very close to the Black Sea. The river ensured that Olbia's inhabitants had abundant pastures and fresh drinking water.[3] The sea further supplemented the inhabitants' diets and increased their access to material goods. Aside from financial riches, the immense level of trade passing through Olbia brought a great wealth of knowledge and a cosmopolitan spirit to the area, which the young Sphaerus was all too eager to soak up. As he stood watching boats load and unload their various cargoes, he yearned to shake off the traditions that no longer served him, and he envisioned the day he would embark on his own journey. He imagined the various people he would

---

* There is very little surviving evidence of Sphaerus' life. With the little we do have, Leo and I have tried to piece together his life's "flow" and, with some evidence-based speculation on our part, get inside Sphaerus' mind and his journey into Stoicism. We have done the same for the Spartan stories in this chapter.

meet along the way, as he fixed his mind's eye on a place that the wisest of travelers he met always seemed to refer to: Athens.

Sphaerus had heard that Athens was the epicenter of learning; it was a place that all seekers of knowledge gravitated toward because this was where the greatest ideas were born, tested, and sent out into the rest of the Hellenic world and beyond. As he envisioned the great men of Athens preparing their speeches, Sphaerus realized that whatever came down the river or blew across the sea was nothing more than secondhand whispers, and he aspired to be in the thick of the action. He promised himself that when he was old enough, he would travel to Athens in the hope of finding a wise teacher who would take him under his wing.

A few years later, while still a young man, Sphaerus made true on his promise by finding a well-weathered mentor in Zeno, who saw in him a youthful version of himself: a fiercely independent pupil of sharp intellect who, having grown up surrounded by merchants trading their wares, lived and breathed the cosmopolitan message. Sphaerus proved to be an excellent student with great initiative. He was brilliant at logic and the defining of philosophical terms.[4] Sphaerus was also keen to take Stoicism beyond the classroom, through the city gates, and out into the world. After all, it wasn't some esoteric philosophy or an exceptionally complex science of the invisible realm that only the dedicated few should trouble themselves with. Rather, Stoicism was about how to experience the "good life," which was something he felt that everyone should be exposed to.

Sphaerus' conviction drove him to deeply consider the real implications of establishing virtue both at the heart of one's personal life and as the bedrock of society. He pored over the tiniest details of Zeno's and Cleanthes' scrolls in the hope that he could master them enough to bring more people along for the journey. He then used his communication skills to transform Zeno's lofty blueprint for the ideal state into a language that educators and re-formers could use.

Sphaerus' first opportunity to teach Stoicism out in the wider world came after Zeno's death, when Pharaoh Ptolemy II requested an audience in Alexandria with Cleanthes, who, due to poor health, sent Sphaerus in his place. While in Egypt, Sphaerus spent a lot of his time polishing his debating skills and writing on various philosophical matters.[5] In particular, he focused on ethics and politics, which furthered his conviction that education wasn't just good for the individual but essential for the making of good citizens. He also studied the works of Heraclitus, a philosopher many Stoics admired because he taught that profound truth is contained in both the ordinary and the mundane, a reality Heraclitus expressed in the phrase, "It is impossible to step in the same river twice." As Sphaerus pondered the meaning behind Heraclitus' message, he realized that when you first step into a river, you are confronted with flowing waters. This means that when you step into the river a second time, the waters you meet are entirely different, and therefore you are not, in fact, stepping into the same river. This is true even if you stand in the same spot. On further consideration, Sphaerus came to appreciate that neither the waters nor the person remains the same. For one thing, the person is older. For another, they experience the waters differently the second time. Right there, it dawned on him that herein lay the power of education: the ability to take a person and help them to see that a hairbreadth increase of knowledge could profoundly alter how they understood themselves and the world around them. The hypnotic nature of Heraclitus' words remained with Sphaerus throughout his entire return journey back to Athens. Once safely through the city's gates, he quietly made himself a promise. He would report to Cleanthes about how he had held his own against the pharaoh and his court, and then he would unroll his scrolls and plan to put more Stoic lessons into action.

Sphaerus, due to Zeno's admiration for the Spartan code of conduct, always felt drawn to Sparta, a city-state that had been historically celebrated for its core values of austerity, discipline, and solidarity. Unfortunately, over the previous century, Sparta had lost these qualities under an oligarchical rule that imposed poverty and suffering upon its people. A particularly insidious policy, squarely aimed at taming the once-fierce Spartan spirit, was the removal of lands and the revoking of citizenship and rights on a whim. Corruption, debt, and decay lingered and led the city to become a shadow of its former self. Sparta, no longer seen as a major player in Greek affairs, was a political ruin. Its education system had crumbled, and its streets had fallen into disrepair. Yet, despite this, and at the risk of upsetting those in charge, Sphaerus felt duty bound to find a way to teach the Spartans something that they had long forgotten — valor, fairness, temperance, and astuteness — the very virtues the Spartan kings and legends of old had held in such high regard.[6]

One of the Spartan kings who didn't quite make the grade for legendary status was Agis IV, whose inability to shine on the battlefield, for lack of opportunity more than anything else, put him at odds with the countless tales of his ancestors' feats that he had been told as soon as he was old enough to sit on his mother's knee. One of his favorite stories involved his grandmother, Archidamia, a particularly strong-willed and principled female leader who taught him the value of never shying away from battle if your principles or your people were on the line. In the story, Archidamia, true to her Spartan spirit and heritage, grabbed her sword in fierce opposition to a fast-approaching invasion led by Pyrrhus of Epirus. Even though Archidamia was encouraged to seek safety by escaping to the nearby island of Crete, she willingly refused. For Agis, such actions personified the toughness of the Spartan backbone and the strength of its citizens' long-held conviction that what was good for Sparta was good for the Spartan. It was this belief that he took forward upon ascending to the throne, and which inspired him to create a comprehensive system of military, economic, legal, land, and educational reforms, in response to unjust oligarchical inequality and mean-spirited extravagance.[7]

By way of example, Agis first applied the spirit of the reforms to himself. He shrugged off his creature comforts and took to wearing an unfashionable coarse Spartan cloak. This personal transformation impressed upon his grandmother, Archidamia, and his mother, Agesistrata, his commitment to the common good — a cause they both joined, despite the fact that Agis called for the confiscation of much of their inherited financial wealth and property!* However, it was much more difficult to convert others and Agis soon found himself chest deep in treacherous waters. He might have been king, and no one's puppet, but he had been wrong to think that he pulled all the strings. In mistakenly believing that the oligarchy would welcome his call to embrace the traditional way of life with open arms, Agis had failed to inform himself of the nature of power and the character of those who pursue it at all costs. It didn't occur to him that Sparta's magistrates, even those he called family and friends, might not be trustworthy! He never stopped to think about the traps they might lay. Yet an educated guess would have told him that those who profited from the status quo were not going to give it up without a fight. Being Spartans, it just wasn't in their nature. Once Agis had been ensnared, it was over all too quickly. His reforms never got off the ground. Worse still, he was denounced, imprisoned, and

---

* Agesistrata and Archidamia were among the richest individuals in Sparta. This was enabled through Spartan laws that, among other things, stated that females inherited even in the presence of male siblings, with a daughter's portion being half that of a son. Spartan women's ability to inherit, possess, and use wealth in their own right had a big impact on, and important implications for, their position in Sparta, as did their education and training.

executed as a "traitor" together with his esteemed grandmother, Archidamia, and his mother, Agesistrata.* Only his wife, Agiatis, and newborn son were spared.

Ironically enough, Agis' efforts to change the world would not go unnoticed, just not in the way he might have imagined or hoped. Of all people, Italian Renaissance philosopher Machiavelli eventually drew attention to Agis' ruin as an example of how *not* to speak truth to power (in *Discourses on Livy* 1.9.4). Interestingly, Machiavelli juxtaposes Agis' failures with the achievements of the later Spartan king, Kleomenes III, who, with the help of Sphaerus and Agis' widow, Agiatis, ruthlessly enacted the economic, legal, land, and educative reforms the Spartan oligarchs so opposed. In the beginning, Kleomenes did not seem like the "lion-fox" that Machiavelli so masterfully depicts, using his example to educate his Renaissance peers on the art of freeing themselves from power struggles and ultimately checkmating their opponent. In part this was because Leonidas II, Kleomenes' own father, was the one who had so deviously led the charge against Agis and his reforms and sentenced Agis to death. Following Agis' removal, Leonidas and his minions needed to quell the whispers of rebellion that had been stirring in the streets ever since the news about the royal murders broke. They also had to ensure that Kleomenes, the young king in waiting, would dance to their tune and not be tempted to stray far from the puppet role they had prepared for him. The linchpin in Leonidas' scheme was the newly widowed Agiatis. Leonidas reasoned that, if he could marry Agiatis off to his son Kleomenes, he would kill not just two, but three, birds with one stone. First, in establishing this alliance, she would cease to be a symbol of resistance for the masses.

---

* In her last act of defiance and in line with Spartan values, and as her head was placed into a noose, Agesistrata uttered, "May this only be of service to Sparta."

Second, her marriage back into royalty would stop her own powerful family from using its immense resources to bring the other oligarchs down. Third, Agiatis would be indebted to Leonidas' mercy, a position he could exploit.

In the early days, Leonidas' plan seemed to work like a charm. Even though Agiatis, out of love and devotion to the memory of her dead husband, Agis, grieved deeply over his demise, she agreed to marry Kleomenes and become his wife. She did her royal duties well and showed genuine affection to Leonidas' son, who equally doted on her. However, Leonidas didn't count on Agiatis' loyalty to Sparta and her commitment to bring Agis' social, political, and educational reforms into fruition. He also severely underestimated her ability to keep the ball firmly in her court and beat him at his own game. Agiatis countered Leonidas' power moves by encouraging Kleomenes to become the hero who would restore Sparta to its former glory. Kleomenes eagerly listened to her, and he often asked her about Agis' character strengths and flaws and his notions for reform.

Before long, Agis' plans became Kleomenes' vision. Knowing the danger and reluctant to lose another spouse to the hangman's rope, Agiatis understood that without wisdom, history would repeat itself. What Kleomenes needed was a prudent mentor. And she knew of only one person equipped for the job: Sphaerus, a man who not only could teach the king the art of reform but would help to sculpt his character so that he would successfully preside over Sparta's new dawn.

On arrival, Kleomenes gave Sphaerus almost free rein over how his plans for Sparta would be put into practice. Kleomenes respected his teacher's judgment and his almost encyclopedic knowledge on Spartan traditions and ideals. He also trusted that Stoicism was the right blade with which to cut out the corruption of the courts and the excesses of the elite. It dawned on Sphaerus that what Kleomenes was really asking for was a restoration of the

Spartan spirit that had once clung like a cape around the proud, broad shoulders of the city's youth. At that moment, both men understood that what was required was nothing short of a revolution, one that would not just overthrow the vicious oligarchy but speak to the Spartan soul. This would take something far more powerful than swords and shields — it would take education. Sphaerus carefully unrolled the scrolls Zeno had left to him, and he got to work by blending the radical ideas of a cosmopolitan utopia with the principles established by the near-mythical ancient Spartan lawgiver Lycurgus.

Zeno and Lycurgus shared one fundamental thing in common; both had consulted the Oracle of Delphi and had subsequently led lives worthy of her advice. Although these two leaders lived five hundred years apart, the Oracle had shared with them the same egalitarian vision built on a bedrock of virtues, held together by mindful discipline and austerity. The Oracle's whispers of prophesy were now, seemingly, speaking to Sphaerus, who could feel his own destiny approaching. From his blueprint for a Stoic education, the need for a strong sense of concord and self-sufficiency emerged, two important qualities he captured in his reestablishment and innovation of the Spartan *agoge*.[8] The latter was a schooling system that essentially created an elite group of warriors who rejected individualism for the sake of the state and the common good. The system's purpose was to train Spartans to live out a disciplined life both on the battlefield and while undertaking their wider civic duties. This just goes to show that there is far more to soldiering excellence than the modern-day Spartan myth would suggest. After all, you didn't have to travel to Sparta to obtain a militarized education, especially given that the Mongols, Huns, and Celts were every bit as ferocious. That's not to say that Sphaerus didn't use Stoic philosophy to prepare the Spartans for when the battlefield was strewn with corpses and the air was filled with the screams of the wounded and dying. He certainly did. But he also emphasized the fact that the rows they were trained to fight in, or phalanx (which literally means "fingers"), were part of one hand, which only functioned correctly when all the fingers worked together.

Sphaerus' teachings also enabled Kleomenes to follow through on all the measures Agiatis had helped him (and Agis) dream up in the name of a stronger Sparta. Laws influenced by Stoicism ensured that non-Spartans had a pathway toward citizenship and that even some of the city's serf class (the helots) were offered a way out of their forced obligation to work the land. This, in turn, allowed a greater number of people to tell their own "Spartan" stories in a way that would be heard and respected. This is why Sphaerus occupies a unique place in the history of philosophy. He proved with outstanding success that you could use philosophically influenced principles at the societal level, not just for the good of the individual but for the common good.

꒩꒩꒩꒩꒩

Chimamanda Ngozi Adichie is a Nigerian novelist who, like Sphaerus, Agis, Kleomenes, and Agiatis, has used her platform and position to inspire social change. She is particularly known for her questioning of, and her open engagement with, ideas that are often considered to be profound truths. Adichie's lessons in the "art of living" weave together simple tales of everyday experience. From a Stoic perspective, Adichie profoundly understands that in order to journey into what Epictetus calls a *true philosophical education*, we must comprehensively and consistently visit and revisit the narratives we form about ourselves and others, especially when they have been condensed into a single story.

Adichie's exposure to the single-story narrative and the way in which it colors, and ultimately distorts, our worldview was something she experienced very early on, when as a seven-year-old she used pencils and crayons to bring to life what stirred in her vivid imagination. Like any child, she was eager to lose herself in the make-believe world she created. Unbeknownst to her at the time, her world was peculiar because it was unlike anything she had, or was likely to, experience. Not because it was full of princesses, monsters, and fairies but because it was made up of white blue-eyed children who bore no resemblance to anyone she had ever met, who ate fruits and drank beverages no one sold, and played with snow that had never fallen in her hometown of Nsukka. As Adichie matured, it dawned on her that the voice she was expressing was not her own. Instead, she was merely echoing the experiences of the white American and British writers whose poetic words were fundamental to her grasp of the English language, yet had, at the same time, convinced her that her own story was not worth telling and that authentic African voices had no audience.

Things changed when she was given a copy of Chinua Achebe's novel *Things Fall Apart*. Its precolonial Nigerian backdrop and its unapologetically African tone not only spoke to her reality but did so in such a way that it invited confidence and gave her permission to peel back the layer of European stories that had masked her innermost thoughts and feelings. This profound shift in Adichie's thinking didn't diminish what she had taken from the anecdotes and insights of well-meaning colonial authors past, but she realized a broader education would put her in better stead as an aspiring author. So she set about teaching herself to be more intentional about the way she weaved her words together. She probed deeper into what is said and what goes unsaid. She reflected on how people remember and think about things. She put her finger on the pulse of war and scrutinized the ways in which some people view and limit the potential of women and Africans in wider society. Full of curiosity, Adichie immersed herself in African literature and the continent's rich history. When she couldn't find the answers to her questions in books, she asked the people she knew difficult questions. She stitched their stories into a striking tapestry that not only captured but celebrated her identity and her experiences as a Nigerian woman. From this fabric Adichie found the threads of her own form of storytelling. Her words resonated with a whole new audience who wanted more than the colonial literary practice of using African characters as a type of scenic furniture or as props supporting the European hero.

Adichie's soulful voice does more than captivate. It challenges the status quo and smashes through the glass ceiling that has held back countless African, female, and black trailblazers. She has helped others shake off the identities that have been imposed on them. When pop artist Beyoncé sampled portions of Adichie's TED Talk "We Should All Be Feminists" in the song *Flawless*, it demonstrated the extent of Adichie's reach, as she unflinchingly questions the value of "teaching girls to shrink themselves" and "to aspire to marriage" when "we don't teach boys the same." Adichie also forces people to confront what it means to be "feminist," a term she defines as "the person who believes in the social, political, and economic equality of the sexes." According to such a definition, Stoics are feminists because of their commitment to justice and their openness to dialogue. Like Adichie, they seek to examine personal and societal perceptions and how they are formed. Only by educating ourselves in this way can we become aware of premises and apparent "facts" that may be false and conclusions that might well be wrong.

The harder we cling to uninformed, or less-informed, opinions, the more difficult it becomes to pivot away and set our own record straight. Eventually, we lose our suppleness and get completely stuck. Over time our life stagnates, and we transform into something so brittle that even the gentlest push against our values and opinions causes us to snap. If we hold on too tightly to unexamined ideals, we end up isolating ourselves to the point that, by limiting our potential for growth, we journey away from *eudaimonia*. We may unwittingly create problems for other people, too, especially if we insist that others restrict their existence to the tiny space between us and what we are unwilling or unable to face or acknowledge. Stoicism leads us to examine the barriers we erect and, where appropriate, to develop the courage to overcome them. In practicing Stoicism, we are required to ask whether our reasons for constructing these barriers are virtuous. Perhaps, we maintain them just because the world has changed away from our liking or, equally, because it will not change *to* our liking. In any case, Stoicism reminds us that when we fence ourselves off from the world, we are ultimately setting ourselves up for failure, precisely because the space we are patrolling becomes an increasingly diminishing comfort zone.

My grandmother, Sheila (who is mentioned in chapter 1), experienced this problem firsthand. As a bookkeeper, she sabotaged her career by stubbornly deciding that computers and spreadsheets were "not for her," long before she had given them a fair chance. By her early fifties, she had effectively written herself out of the job market. Her aversion to computers was such that it had caused her to resign every time the prospect of computerized accounting loomed. This painful pattern continued for years, until, finally, she had the good fortune of being offered a part-time position by a boss who, like her, hadn't yet embraced this "new" technology and was happy for her to do the company's payroll using pen and paper.

Sheila stayed in this job for over a decade and didn't train herself on computers in the meantime. It never occurred to her that she would have to use a computer prior to her retirement. The world had other ideas, and it wasn't long before the British government requested that all payroll be digitized and submitted online. Sheila had to face the fact that she had to either get with the times or never work again. On deeper reflection, she realized that she wanted to work because of the sense of purpose and financial freedom it gave her. The thought of losing those things frightened her more than sitting in front of a computer. Once she made the decision to overcome her fears, her family and work colleagues rallied around her. This reassured her that she was still valued at work and that, despite her age, she still had something to offer her employer. With a newfound sense of determination, Sheila did the unthinkable. She signed up for a basic computing course at the local library. She had a mountain to climb. Even remembering to log off and shut down the computer correctly, instead of straightforwardly pushing the off button, created a sense of panic. Simply opening an internet page and typing in the correct web address was stressful, since she believed that just one spelling mistake might cause the computer to crash. Her daughters encouraged her to write down the sequences she needed to remember. Armed with a pack of sticky notes and a pen, she made slow progress and eventually earned a certificate in computer literacy. After that, she learned digital bookkeeping. This might not seem like much to an outsider, but it represented a big milestone for Sheila, who, once again, had to expand her comfort zone and horizon. Not only did she successfully extend her working life, but she experienced the unexpected joy of communicating with her grandchildren and friends on social media. She also used the internet to book the leisure trips that, ultimately, her decision to keep her part-time job afforded her.

Like a river, life does not stand still, and our education remains ongoing. The principle "Only the educated are free" embodies a continual search for wisdom and a perpetual questioning in order to know what to do or not to do and how best to succeed. No one finishes their education — not philosophers, highly acclaimed novelists, college professors, schoolteachers, or scientists — because no one is immune from foolishness or even outright ignorance. With this principle as our foundation, we free ourselves from the bondage of our own unthinking impulses, strong emotions, and unyielding certainties. As Sphaerus taught, we can learn to go beyond what some might call self-development by becoming good citizens. In part, that means taking the time to listen to other people's stories and to reflect on our own. Among other things, this Stoic practice may provide us with new perspectives that can enrich our experience and encourage us to keep moving forward in own journey toward *eudaimonia*.

SPHAERUS' QUESTIONS

In Stoicism, learning involves action. It is not a passive experience. It is not enough to memorize theory in a classroom. You have to take the lessons learned and practice them in the real world. That's why Sphaerus felt so strongly about traveling to Sparta. His Stoic education meant so much more to him when it was used for the common good.

- What are the key issues and problems that affect your community and how can you educate yourself further about them? How do your local issues relate to society in general or the bigger picture?

- Once you have a better sense of your community's reality, how are you going to respond to the local issues you and your community face? Are there reasons why you can't or wouldn't respond to these issues?

CHAPTER 8

LIVE ACCORDING
TO NATURE

[The objective of life is] to live contemplating the truth and order of
all things together and helping in promoting it as far as possible,
in no way being led by the irrational part of the soul.
— Posidonius, as cited by Clement of Alexandria, *Stromateis* 2.21[1]

Arguably, no Stoic epitomizes the quest for wisdom more
than Posidonius, a Greek from Apamea in Syria, who studied under Panaetius (see chapter 5). Like his mentor, Posidonius
was particularly interested in the practical elements of Stoicism that
could help his students navigate the world in a virtuous manner.
His thirst for knowledge led him to search far and wide for answers
to life's biggest questions, which he discovered by peeling back the
mysteries of the universe one theory and science experiment at a
time. That said, his life's work wasn't just a scientific pursuit but a
dedicated and respectful journey into the very mind of God.

Posidonius' desire to intimately understand God's essence
launched him on a trailblazing journey that left no stone un-
turned. During one fact-finding mission, the people of Gaul gave
him detailed insights into the movements of the celestial bodies
and the tides. They also shared with him their beautiful recitals
and introduced him to their priestly caste, the Druids, who enjoyed discussing investigations into natural causes, physical phe-
nomena, and the makings of the soul.

Posidonius' adventurous spirit provided him with countless stories that he drew on to teach Stoic theory. It also endeared him to many in the upper echelons of Roman society. His friends in high places included various leading figures of the late Roman Republic, including the statesman Cicero (see chapter 3) and the military and political leader Pompey. Cicero and Pompey came to his lectures on Stoicism, and their thoughts and actions often reflected Stoic teachings. Both men admired their mentor's strict adherence to Stoic principles and the way in which he embodied them. Posidonius had a particularly interesting relationship to pain, which he would not allow to get the better of him. On one occasion, when suffering from gout, he quipped: "It's no good, pain; bothersome you may be, but you will never persuade me that you are an evil" (as recorded in Cicero's *Tusculan Disputations* 2.25). Pompey and Cicero were so impressed with Posidonius' response that they continually reminded each other of the episode. Eventually, Cicero wrote it down so that others could follow the example set by the man he considered to be the "greatest of all Stoics."[2]

Pompey was, perhaps, influenced by Posidonius to an even greater extent than Cicero. Following his mentor's advice, he took more humane courses of action during his military campaigns in the East. For example, at one point, rather than execute a group of defeated pirates, Pompey negotiated a treaty that led to their resettlement and retraining. This drew the ire of many Romans, including Cicero, who disliked Stoic war strategies involving pardoning and rehabilitation, even if such a response was more likely to prevent further bloodshed and theft. The unpopularity of Pompey's reasoning didn't seem to sway him because, having calculated the risk, Pompey was convinced that his conciliatory tone would strike a chord with the troublemakers. In any case, he very much wanted to be liked by Posidonius and enjoyed the idea of being associated with his teacher's cosmopolitan ideals and thought process.[3]

Posidonius was revered throughout the Greco-Roman world not only for his Stoicism but also for his prolific contributions to anthropology, astronomy, botany, geography, history, hydrology, mathematics, meteorology, seismology, and zoology. His list of admirers was considerable and, apart from Cicero and Pompey, included the Stoic Roman statesman Seneca the Younger,[4] the Roman physician Galen, the Greek geographer and historian Strabo, and the Greek mathematician and astronomer Ptolemy. The different backgrounds of those who cited Posidonius' work attested to his breadth and depth of knowledge, which grew along with his insatiable drive to create his own "theory of everything."[5]

For Posidonius, nothing was more important than knowing how the world worked and nothing was more useful than a perfectly complementary scientific and philosophical approach to life.* In his classroom, he taught animatedly on how a thoroughly fact-based understanding of the world was the only lens through which our thoughts, actions, and roles in society become clear. Posidonius prized freethinking. He had no qualms about reconsidering and rewriting the conclusions reached by earlier Stoics on all matters of inquiry, especially when he thought, as he did quite frankly, that they had not put the same amount of time and effort into investigating the natural sciences.

Yet Posidonius did not change things merely for the sake of it. Rather, he was careful about blending and balancing innovation with long-held, standing traditions, so as to create a coherent and

---

* The philosopher Immanuel Kant, who was inspired by Stoicism, shares similar sentiments in his *Critique of Practical Reason* when he writes: "Two things fill the mind with ever new and increasing admiration and awe, the more often and steadily we reflect upon them: the starry heavens above me and the moral law within me."

consistent body of Stoic knowledge. His harmonious approach to Stoic philosophy mirrored his belief in what is now referred to as the "traditional Stoic worldview." This represents a complex mix of pantheism (the belief that Nature is God) and theism (a belief in the existence of a supreme being or beings).[6] A modern articulation of this worldview is expressed by renowned primatologist Frans de Waal:

> The way our bodies are...influenced by surrounding bodies is one of the mysteries of human existence, but one that provides the glue that holds entire societies together....We occupy nodes within a tight network that connects all of us in both body and mind.[7]

What de Waal calls "glue," Posidonius and Cicero[8] called the *logos*. Stoics understand the *logos* to be the perfectly rational and benevolent nature of the universe that pervades all elements of life and thus links and holds everything together in its causal web.* The *logos* also provides the foundation of humankind's rational nature and mandates what "excellent" behavior consists of. It is, consequently, thought to be the very reason that everything exists and operates the way it does, and it is responsible for the varying capacities humans, other animals, and plants have to communicate and collaborate with one another.

Stoics revered Nature and the providential care it provides because of this intrinsic connection between being at one with the universe and the ability to lead the "good life." This vision of Nature as the giver and sustainer of life is what drove Posidonius to dig deeper. With each new and more detailed observation, he saw himself drawing ever closer to the Divine, which he (and

---

* It is "benevolent" in the sense that Nature generously provides all that is sufficient and necessary for life to not only continue but prosper.

the Stoics generally) understood to be the perfect rationality that reveals itself in the patterns and processes of the natural world. Spurred on by his discoveries, Posidonius became increasingly convinced that the essence of God was apparent in every blade of grass, in every note a bird sings, and in every intricate movement of the celestial bodies (which were often referred to as gods in Stoic theory and Roman writings generally).

Posidonius' systematic research into natural philosophy and the natural sciences breathed new life into Stoic physics (the study of the natural world, which also included metaphysics). He fundamentally changed the way Stoics thought about their relationships with plants, animals, and the universe as a whole.[9] For one thing, Posidonius did not make a hard distinction between humans and other animals (Chrysippus was much more adamant in his belief in inherent differences). Instead, and based on his observations, Posidonius believed that the irrational tendencies of humans mirrored, certainly more than we would care to admit, the behavior expressed by other animals and even plants!

While Posidonius accepted that the capacity for rationality allowed humans to better understand and cooperate with the cosmos, he also saw that most people gave in too easily to their base desires and the "emotional pulls" of their own idiosyncratic nature. He believed this behavior made them miserable because in falling back into vice — cowardice, injustice, greed, and ignorance — they misaligned themselves with God's own nature and providential purposes. In this regard, were he alive today, Posidonius would be neither shocked nor surprised by the world's heavily subsidized, fossil fuel–based economy, which continues to devastate the natural world. He would not be astonished that so many people continue to advocate for the dirty technologies that undermine Nature's ability to care for all beings. After all, his observations had already confirmed the reckless abandon and selective blindness that we humans indulge in when we defend the irrational side of the soul — that is, when we value and chase wealth, health, and status — rather than the four Stoic virtues of courage, justice, self-control, and wisdom.

Posidonius, in trying to account for how the world works, frequently argued against myth and superstition in favor of rational explanations that could be understood through cause and effect. His various travels led him to assert that there was enough wonder in the world without the need for a belief in magic. For this reason, he reinterpreted the Stoic motto "Live according to Nature" to be, as quoted in the chapter-opening epigraph: "to live contemplating the truth order of all things together and...in no way being led by the irrational part of the soul." He argued that this could be done if people were trained to exercise the mind's rational capacities. This practice involves the habitual and purposeful recalibration of irrational responses (including those that trigger extreme emotions) by accepting, on evidence, that we are part of the world, inseparable from it, and that we can only take care of ourselves by taking care of our planet.

In Stoicism, to "Live according to Nature" means that we have an obligation to live in harmony with the natural world, though the exact way we do depends on many factors, including our age, where we live, our occupation, likes and dislikes, and so on. For instance, for a Muslim who prays five times a day, the Stoic approach would be to personally practice the religion in an environmentally considerate way. However, even better would be to have a collective vision and engage in the raising of funds that bring the Muslim community together to build a sustainable mosque.

This is what was done by Abdal Hakim Murad — the globally renowned University of Cambridge scholar, who is also known as Tim Winter. Murad and his team led the fundraising, designing, and building of Cambridge Central Mosque, in Cambridge, England, which is Europe's first purpose-built, environmentally friendly, Islamic place of worship.[10] Aside from its eco-design aspects — including solar panels, natural ventilation, rainwater harvesting, a green roof, bird boxes, and sustainable timber construction — the environmental harmony of the mosque transcends religion. Within the mosque and its surrounding garden are frequent references to the Divinity that Muslims revere when they reflect upon the Quranic verse (Al-Baqarah 2:115), "And to Allah belongs the east and the west. So, wherever you might turn, there is the Face of Allah."

By focusing on and celebrating the universality and the sanctity of the natural world, the mosque was designed to fully embrace and provide an example of how Islamic worship can more deeply connect to the oneness of the Divine. As Posidonius himself understood, the natural world is a huge art gallery that embodies the power and providential character of God, and which, consequently, is worthy of our care, consideration, and respect. From an Islamic perspective, deeper connections with the natural world invoke a transformative understanding of how Allah's all-encompassing breath is made manifest in the patterns and the tiniest details of the universe. Such connections are also captured in the frequency of Islamic prayer (*salah*) and the monthlong fast of Ramadan. Both these tenets embed a Muslim's spiritual practice firmly in the dynamics of the local community and in the physical reality of that location. The timings of the five daily prayers occur in response to the motion of Earth relative to the sun, while the start and end of Ramadan are marked by the physical sighting of the moon. There are also special (and quite lengthy) communal prayers following a solar or lunar eclipse, one of the many signs that Muslims believe Allah uses to reveal His presence. In this respect, as the Stoics would concur, living according to Nature is very much about understanding and responding to the reality of where you are (both figuratively and geographically) and undertaking your roles and responsibilities accordingly.

For Abdal Hakim Murad and his team, the mosque's construction represented an opportunity to express a distinctly British identity that is deeply rooted in the Islamic tradition, while avoiding any cultural trappings that might emphasize difference, promote exclusivism, or be seen as acts of defiance. The desire for a harmonious and uplifting experience, particularly in the prayer hall, led to frequent consultations with local people, whose ideas and concerns were incorporated in the award-winning design. Classically Islamic and yet characteristically English, the mosque incorporates stained-glass windows and yew hedges, which would not look out of place in the many Anglican churches and churchyards dotted around the English countryside.

This architectural vision has meant that local non-Muslim residents do not find the mosque to be an imposing building. Instead, they feel it integrates with and promotes their cultural values, enhances their immediate surroundings, and respects their sensitivities.* Likewise, the local Muslim community, and the many visitors who come from far and wide to enjoy the space, are proud of what has been achieved from an environmental perspective. They appreciate the attention to detail and the openness and accessibility of the facility, which is designed for all ages, all

---

* One particularly evident concession is that the mosque does not have a minaret. However, a minaret would serve no practical purpose in this case, as the mosque's call to prayer is not broadcast outside of its walls. Further, Islamic standards do not require a minaret, since the first mosque (the Prophet's mosque) did not have one.

genders, and those who are less able-bodied, who often find themselves unable to frequent places of worship. Precisely because the mosque is a source of welcome and spiritual renewal, both Muslims and non-Muslims, local residents and visitors, enjoy the mosque, which — through its building, grounds, and message — reminds everyone, just like the Stoic principle, that we must not live at odds with Nature.

ꙂꙂꙂꙂꙂ

Contemplating and promoting truth requires that we rigorously and purposefully take steps to uncover it. This undertaking might lead us to enroll in a specific university course or to borrow books from a particular shelf in the library, but it is just as likely to cause us to sit up and take notice in our local park or even our own garden. In any case, harmonizing our lifestyle with natural processes involves active engagement, not just abstract thinking. It doesn't necessarily have to stem from an overtly religious or spiritual practice. Zeno and Chrysippus were particularly adamant that a temple was not needed to experience or revere the Divine. On the contrary, Stoics believe that being outside among rivers, mountains, and forests is how we most readily cultivate attitudes that are in harmony with Nature and where we best reflect upon, and draw closer to, God.

In the Stoic tradition, the essence of Nature (the *logos*) permeates throughout the entire universe. It is present in every human, animal, plant, and rock. It is the most complete expression of virtue; a oneness characterized by providential order, structure, and wholeness. It follows that if virtue is our goal and Posidonius, in particular, is our role model, then Nature (as a whole, and not any specific animal, plant, or rock) has intrinsic value and is worth observing, respecting, understanding, and imitating to the best of our ability. This, in turn, underscores the transformative power of purposefully spending our time, and engaging our skill sets, to understand and appreciate how all life has been fashioned together in order to reveal the pattern of the universe — regardless of how we believe the universe was made, either by God or through mechanistic, physical processes.

Seeking unity with the natural world, by extending our care toward animals, plants, and their habitats, helps us to reevaluate our priorities and reconfigure our values. If we are spiritually or religiously inclined, as Epictetus and Cleanthes were, we might revere Nature in similar ways to the Sufi teacher Hazrat Inayat Khan, who frequently reflected on "the sacred manuscript of nature, the only scripture which can enlighten the reader."[11] If we prefer Zeno's and Chrysippus' more agnostic/atheistic inclination, we might simply revel in the melodies of the forest as we try to distinguish one bird's song from another. Either way, a Stoic's appreciation of Nature goes beyond taking selfies and a superficial enjoyment of breathtaking sights and sounds. It involves a profound thirst for the kind of knowledge that helps us understand how the world works and our position within it.

Through this deep relationship with the Divine we can challenge the perceived role of consumerism in our own sense of happiness, especially when what we consume contributes to the obliteration of pristine rain forests, coral reefs, and cherished landscapes. Thinking more conscientiously about virtue and the journey we are on can help us to make wiser decisions about those attitudes and actions that exacerbate pollution, environmental damage, and climate breakdown. Leo and I believe that the present environmental crisis represents the biggest threat to humanity's ability to flourish. After all, how can our children hope to achieve what Zeno referred to as the "good life" if the air is so polluted that their brains do not develop properly? How can they think well if they don't have clean water to drink? Is it fair that some people enjoy gas-guzzling SUVs and meat-heavy diets (and their excessive carbon emissions) if this leads to burning forests and rising sea levels and global temperatures, which destroy the homes of other people and their ability to grow crops?

Deeply questioning our role in society and our impact upon Earth and its natural processes led Leo and me to expand Hierocles' original circles of concern (see chapter 6) to encompass the environment. By introducing this circle into Stoic theory and practice, we want to capture humankind's connection to the living Earth, since the environment sustains and supports the self, families, society, and all living beings. Leo and I also want to highlight humankind's moral obligation to act on behalf of plants, animals, and the planet generally, in ways that ensure our collective well-being. This is now even more imperative given that, through intensive fossil-fuel extraction and mass deforestation, for example, people have negated or sufficiently reduced Nature's ability to offer the providential care that enables the planet to flourish.[12] In this regard, the extension of the circles of concern (see page 120) serves as a graphic reminder of the fundamentally Stoic call to strive for the courage, justice, self-control, and wisdom required to tackle the environmental crisis. In line with Hierocles' instructions, we are required to bring each successive circle back upon the previous one. This would lead us to treat our family members like ourselves, our friends as if they were family, and so on, until eventually we see Nature's essence in us and our individual selves as part of the web that constitutes the cosmos. The "Earth" circle also reminds us that when we harmonize our thoughts and actions with Nature, we are very much building upon the lessons taught to us by the ancient Stoics.

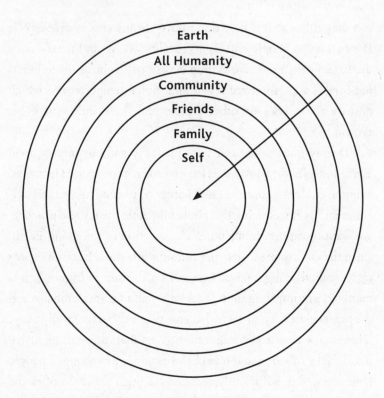

The extended circles of concern

Environmentalism is not something that should be restricted to politicians (who haven't done a particularly good job), political activists, or philosophers. Everyone should play their part in helping to secure a more sustainable (and consequently virtuous) path forward. For Stoics, this means acting in ways that are appropriate to the four roles (which includes one's circumstances and preferences). For example, a musician could engage people with environmentally conscious lyrics; a religious leader could introduce environmental concerns into their sermons. Teachers could grapple with sustainability issues in their lesson plans, and fine artists could incorporate environmental themes in their canvases and sculptures. Chefs and restaurants could source their products from local farms, feature seasonal fruits and vegetables in their dishes, and share knowledge of these practices with diners. Even a car mechanic could do their bit for the planet by minimizing the environmental impact of their business by thinking about the appropriateness of repairing rather than replacing certain car parts, for example.

In any role, when you pledge to do the right thing for the right reason, it will involve an investment on your part. This may include taking more time to weigh potential solutions, talking them over with people you trust, and even paying a little more money for a more ethically sound option.[13] Once you are better informed about the available choices, go one step further and ask which ones stand up to the scrutiny of a reasoned argument and exemplify the "right thing." For instance, take the hypothetical example of a singer trying to make a living in the music business while promoting an environmental message. The singer should think not just about the lyrics in their songs but the way they conduct every aspect of their business. Do they try to minimize carbon emissions when they go on tour, and do they try to play at venues that do the same? Conversely, what message would it send if they sing about green values but lead an excessively materialistic lifestyle and actively encourage fans to mimic this and follow them as they globetrot from venue to venue, flying around the world? People watch what we do and listen carefully to what we say, and so if a singer does not live the life they promote in their music, their environmental songs become no more than virtue-signaling their "green" credentials.

This same dynamic applies to everyone. From a Stoic perspective, we should take the circles of concern seriously and consider how they apply throughout our lives and within all our relationships. We should think very carefully about the appropriateness of our lifestyle choices to make sure they are consistent with our values. Stoicism is not about doing the impossible or trying to singlehandedly solve complex social or environmental issues. It's about consistently doing what you can within the life you lead using the personality, knowledge, social role, network, and skill set that you already have.

࿏࿏࿏࿏࿏

A can-do attitude epitomizes Tom Rahill's Swamp Apes, a nonprofit organization in Florida that facilitates the positive reintegration of US veterans back into civilian life through environmental conservation. Swamp Apes' mission is twofold. Its primary purpose is to help restore the health of the Floridian Everglades, which has declined significantly following the introduction and proliferation of various invasive species, particularly the Burmese python and other introduced reptiles. The exotic pest problem began in earnest following Hurricane Andrew in 1992, which among other things severely damaged a reptile breeding facility. Many of its residents escaped, and in the absence of natural predators or competition, they thrived in their new environment.

This biodiversity issue is compounded by the frequent release of unwanted exotic pets by irresponsible owners who have grown bored of, or no longer have the physical or economic capacity to look after, their unusual family members. Illegal pet releases, aside from causing harm to the individual animal, bring into question the wisdom (never mind the ethics) of buying and selling exotic species for the pet market in the first place.

Burmese pythons, in particular, have left a huge path of destruction in their wake. Native populations of midsize mammals, including marsh rabbits, bobcats, and raccoons, have rapidly declined because they have no natural defense against such a large threat. Their ability to survive is also substantially reduced because pythons have a voracious appetite and will continue to indiscriminately swallow up prey until they are filled to the brim. Over the course of a few weeks, a python can eat a lot of animals, especially if the snake in question is fifteen feet long!

The sheer size and reproductive ability of pythons has made it very difficult for Floridian wildlife authorities to effectively manage them. In most cases, python removal from the Everglades requires night hunts involving considerable treks over uneven and almost inaccessible terrain. Few people have the specific skill set and mindset required to tackle a wild python, which isn't venomous but is known for its powerful jaws and needle-sharp teeth. Hunting pythons can be particularly dangerous and, for many, somewhat frightening. The job requires situational awareness and an ability to function well in high-stress, high-threat environments.

The idea for what became Swamp Apes occurred to Tom Rahill following a spiritual epiphany that led him to abstain from alcohol and embrace Christianity. He wondered how best to use his skills and abilities to impact the lives of people while simultaneously improving the environment. For him, the all-important question was how to combine these two missions in a way that mirrored the mercy, love, and stewardship he read about in the Bible. As he considered the role he could play in his local community, he realized that, on the one hand, Florida had a python problem, and on the other, it was home to many veterans whose specialized skills and mental fortitude were undervalued in civilian life. Tom knew many ex-soldiers were burdened and burned out, rather than enriched, by their lives following separation from the armed forces, and he wanted to help them.

Rahill became convinced that he could put people's military training and various other positive attributes to good use. All he had to do was give veterans a chance to recapture and reconnect with themselves in a way that talking to a therapist couldn't. The more steps Rahill took toward making his dream a reality, the more sure-footed he felt. After all, who better than veterans to combat a snake invasion?

Along with countless other ex-military personnel (30 percent of them women), Leo has participated in Swamp Apes and found solace in the Everglades. Swamp Apes has helped him and many others to regain a sense of appreciation for their survival and combat skills by offering a way to reengage with the more positive aspects of the soldiering experience. Every time Leo pulls on his boots and repositions his head torch, he gives himself another opportunity to build character, especially resilience. He also gets to learn more about the nuances of Nature and stay in touch with members of the veteran community, who often understand one another in ways that those who have never served might not.

For some, the impact of Swamp Apes has been profound. While the python hunts are not intended as a form of clinical or psychiatric intervention, they have acted as recreational therapy. They have provided respite from some of the most intrusive and debilitating symptoms of post-traumatic stress disorder (PTSD). This, in turn, has facilitated an emotional reconnection to family members, a restored sense of purpose, and an ability to nurture trust. Together, all these benefits have improved the participants' well-being.[14] They have also highlighted, in Rahill's own words, "the value of serving veterans through serving the wilderness."

For Stoics, virtue happens when our character is perfectly aligned with Nature, as demonstrated by our firm and unyielding conviction that we are doing all that lies within our power to think and act prudently, bravely, moderately, and justly. Understanding our role in relation to the world around us requires that we look through life using two lenses. The first is a microscope that allows us to see, and change accordingly, the tiniest of details that improve or distort the virtuous aspects of our character. The second is a telescope, which enables us to recognize the universal patterns that indicate that we are just one of the many creatures who reside in the cosmos and belong to the universal community held together by the Divine Whole. This doesn't require religious belief or even spirituality. Like Posidonius, if you simply seek the truth, you will find that this *is* the path to *eudaimonia*. After all, how can you be courageous, just, self-controlled, and wise if you are not looking for the truth?

POSIDONIUS' QUESTIONS

The ability to reach *eudaimonia* depends on your capacity to reason. Reason is sharpened by your efforts to understand the nature of the universe and your position within it. Superstition and mistaken ideas about how the world works will not serve you well. In fact, they will give you the wrong impression about what you should do and how you should do it. If you believe the sun rises in the west and sets in the east, and you refuse to consider anything else, then the evidence of every day will upset you, and nothing will alleviate your troubled life.

- Have you ever been asked to believe in something that you deemed to be false? Did you call out that falsehood, or was "not rocking the boat" more important than truth? Since truth is important, how can you reconcile what you feel inside with what is expected of you or what you have come to expect of yourself?

- In what ways is your life, and/or your spiritual journey, intertwined with Nature and the environment? Do you feel your actions and lifestyle support what's essential in that relationship? How might you improve it?

CHAPTER 9

WELL ON THE WAY
TO A LIFE TRANSFORMED...

Zeno died in the following way. As he was leaving the school, he tripped and broke his finger. Smiting the ground with his hand, he uttered, "I am coming. Why do you call for me?" and died instantly by holding his breath.

— Diogenes Laertius, *Lives of the Eminent Philosophers* 7.28–29[1]

The first step of Zeno's journey occurred once he learned to let go of his precious cargo of dye, which ended up at the bottom of the Aegean Sea. The last took place when he decided that his aging body and slowing mind would no longer support his progress toward the "good life." Given what we know about the human body, it is difficult to imagine that even Zeno had so much control over his respiratory functions that he could effectively cause his own death by choosing not to breathe. The fact that those who knew him (or knew of him) celebrated his ability to control death (even if it wasn't true) tells us something about how they viewed his sense of discipline and the dignity of his approach to *eudaimonia*.

Does Zeno's decision to peacefully end his own life make you feel uncomfortable? Or is it disappointing that Zeno so willingly gave up the gift of life that God (the *logos*) presented to him? Does it seem wise for anyone to decide when it is time to go? Many people want to live for as long as possible, and there is a widespread, social aversion toward euthanasia. However, whatever you feel, in the Stoic view, each person must decide for themselves what to do in the face of death, if that is at all possible.

Life is simply the canvas upon which we paint. As with art, the way we apply the brushstrokes, the colors we use, and the scene we draw are what give our work value and meaning. In other words, what we do with our life is what matters, which is why the Stoics were interested in teaching us *how* to live, which includes *how* to approach death. For instance, do we choose to treat people justly when we are healthy and rely on no one? Do we do the same when we are sick and dependent on the kindness of others? Do we seek wisdom, even when it may contradict our deeply held convictions about who we are and how the world works? Or do we instead cling to the unexamined beliefs of our childhood or early adulthood? Are we content to uncritically accept and follow others' instructions because we want to fit in? Or do we find the courage to forge our own path? The "good life" requires that we ask ourselves difficult questions and work through our answers. It involves reflecting upon when and how we are acting out the four virtues of courage, justice, self-control, and wisdom.

When we decide to take the Stoic journey, what happens? First, we come to appreciate that most of what we and others think is important falls far short of what really matters in life (and death). In light of this, we begin to trace our own path from Zeno's Painted Porch toward *eudaimonia*. As we consider the two-thousand-year-old Stoic legacy, we work its principles into our own life, which leads us to understand that virtue is the only good and that everything else is little more than baggage we cling to.

Venturing down this narrower path takes us away from the paved main road of materialistic desire and the unequivocal acceptance of unhealthy family or work-based values. We learn to turn our back on the need to instantly please or appease ourselves and others. As a result, we become less bothered by what other people think of us (or what we think they think about us), and instead we give ourselves permission to pause and reflect. We start to see beyond our own desires for instant gratification and set our sights on what we actually want: a life in harmony with our inner thoughts, our community, and the environment.

As this journey toward *eudaimonia* continues, we arrive at a point where we stop comparing ourselves to others. Perhaps we stop repeating over and over, "Why do I keep making the same mistakes?" or, "Why is it so much easier for everyone else?" Instead, we ask ourselves, "Is this what a wise person would do?" or, "Is this what a wise person would see as fair?" Eventually, we follow these questions with the affirmation, "I am going to set out to do what a wise person would do," and then we act in ways that demonstrate this commitment, which is a victory in and of itself.

As we break cycles of destructive thoughts, we open up enough mental space to pay attention to an altogether subtler sound: the whisper of the *logos*, which pervades all elements of life and mandates what "excellent" behavior consists of. Like Sphaerus, Zeno, and countless other Stoics, we might not hear the *logos* speak to us straight away. However, as long as we willingly do our part for the common good, we will be able to envision our destiny. We *will* be able to transform our personal life and the lives of others (including those of animals) in such a way that it gives us a sense of inner stillness. Speaking personally, Leo and I do not experience this state of being all the time, or even every day, but we do feel it increasingly often, and we have Stoicism to thank for it.

It can be hard to let go of vice and not be drawn into the herd mentality. We are a social species programmed to look for social clues as to how to behave. That does not mean that we should withdraw to our (Epicurean) garden, lock the gate, and never venture out again. A Stoic is someone who actively engages with the world because there is no virtue in hiding. A Stoic doesn't just sit around hoping not to get sucked up into the vortex of other people's vices and of global events. They know that things like earthquakes, wars, pandemics, and climate-related disasters will come to their door, which is why they work on strengthening their character when things are easy and when things are hard.

In 2020, the character of the world's seven billion people was tested by what can only be described as the catastrophic events and consequences of the Covid-19 pandemic. In fact, as we write this, both Leo and I have spent months in voluntary confinement at home, trying, like most of the world's population, to flatten the infection curve, giving our health services the time and support they need to fight this disease. During lockdown, we have seen some of the best and worst of human behavior. We have seen supermarket shelves stripped due to excessive hoarding — as well as witnessed people profiting financially from the crisis — to the point that frontline staff couldn't obtain basic foodstuffs after a long shift caring for the sick. Yet, equally, we have seen a considerable number of retirees, trainees, refugees, and everyday citizens offer their skills and time to assist others.* For every politician who has downplayed the virus for political gain or sheer greed, millions of ordinary people have helped neighbors who are unable to collect their groceries or emotionally cope with the social restrictions put in place. For every irresponsible person who has selfishly flaunted temporary curfews and refused to wear masks, millions more have followed safety guidelines, practiced social distancing, and clapped on their doorsteps and out of their windows in a collective show of appreciation for the caregivers and

---

* In the United Kingdom, for example, more than 405,000 members of the general public offered to volunteer for the National Health Service (NHS) within twenty-four hours of the call being made.

health workers who are risking their lives. The selfless dedication of many doctors, nurses, and support staff has been inspiring,* given that they work long, grueling shifts, risk infection themselves, and some even have died on their feet, having refused to take beds from other potentially sick patients. We will not forget them.

These examples of the best and worst behavior of humankind, once again, remind us that it is not our present circumstances or the direness of our situation that causes misery, but instead how we respond to them. Even amid a pandemic or a war, we can strive to make the right choices for the right reasons. As long as we remain in control of our mental faculties, even if we are sick, even as we lay dying, we can still seek virtue and not fall back into vice.

Though few of us like to admit it, we are all approaching death. This realization is not something that should frighten or startle us. Dying is no evil, nor even a bad thing, because its very existence provides us with a sense of urgency and direction. Death is something that should encourage us to act in ways that we will ultimately find fulfilling. In any case, death is not something we can escape, nor does it have any bearing on the kind of person we want to be. As Marcus Aurelius said (*Meditations* 2.11[2]):

> Death and life, fame and obscurity, wealth and poverty happen to good and bad people in equal measure, being neither right or wrong in themselves and so they are neither good nor bad.

Given that death tells us nothing about a person's character, nor the lessons we can learn from them, there is relatively little

---

* In May 2020, Banksy, the British graffiti artist, created a drawing of a child playing with a nurse action figure, having thrown away his superheroes, that captures the British opinion of the NHS generally, but especially during the pandemic.

to be achieved in focusing too much on how a person died. On the contrary, there is much benefit in thinking deeply about how a person lived. In this book, we have shared the stories of great men and women who have taught us that happiness lies in living virtuously and harmoniously with those around us and the planet. Death does not take away the lessons we learned from our heroes, for it does not prevent their deeds from living on in the minds and works of others — a fact Isaac Newton reflected on when he wrote, "If I have seen further, it is only by standing on the shoulders of giants."[3]

With Newton's words in mind, Leo and I invite you to build a set of shoulders others can stand on. As Epictetus alludes to in his *Discourses* (1.4.13–14), it is not what the weights look like (or indeed how expensive they are) that makes the difference. What matters is how effectively you train and how far you are willing to push yourself so that your mind, body, and surroundings improve.

Yes, life is short and finite. And, yes, just like us, you will have to decide how best to fill the space between today and your last day. To do this effectively, you will need to choose virtue daily, breaking down your choices into a series of steps that might not mean much on their own but taken together will constitute your journey toward *eudaimonia*. Thankfully, our ability to follow this path does not worsen with age.[4] Rather, it waxes and wanes in line with our desire to live virtuously. Staying on the path is not about never getting knocked down, but rather about how quickly we recover when things go awry.[5] Regardless of how old we are (or feel), the issue is not that we have too little time but that we waste so much of it. The ancient Stoics believed that life provides us with plenty of opportunities to learn that frustration, jealousy, and anger effectively shorten the time we have on Earth. Virtue does not exist in a vacuum, and therefore it cannot be contained in the mind of the person who works on being better. Instead, a virtuous action is like a stone thrown into a lake — the impact causes a ripple effect that extends far and wide, touching shores that can't be seen. This is why Stoicism isn't really about personal development but rather the effort made to know who you are and what you must do to create a harmonious world.

For Leo and me, herein lies the success of Stoicism — the ability to recognize that you alone have the power to seek and journey onto a life transformed. A life where success is not marked by riches or poverty, anonymity or fame, physical ability or disability, but by the decision to strive for *eudaimonia*, that is to say, for a life worthy of being lived and for a world worth living in.

ZENO'S QUESTIONS

Death is not a bad thing, but it is final. Therefore, we should focus on how we live so that, regardless of when and how we die, we are at peace with ourselves and others.

- Imagine your own obituary. What would it say about you? What do you want people to remember about you?

ACKNOWLEDGMENTS

While Leo and I have our names on the cover of this book, it is a product of more than our thoughts and words. Unsurprisingly, there are many people who helped us make *Being Better* what it is.

First and foremost, we are grateful to the ancient and contemporary Stoics, some of whom we wrote about here, others we hope to tell you about in our next book, and some whose names and stories have been lost to the shifting sands of time. We are indebted to all those people, ancient and modern, who have worked to make Stoicism an important and relevant philosophical school. We also would like to thank all the non-Stoics whose stories we tell. We are pleased to do our part to ensure that their admirable actions inspire others to do the right thing for the right reason.

In particular, Leo and I would like to thank Abdal Hakim Murad, the Cambridge Central Mosque community, and Tom Rahill and his team at Swamp Apes for their generosity and support. We would also like to thank the team of readers who shaped our thoughts and the text. A special thanks to Dawn Branigan and Gabriel Carmona (without whom this book would have been much more difficult to write); Gail and Mary for their English language comments; and Eddie Simpson, Andrew King, Hanna Murray-Carlsson, Peter Fay, Mexi Sandoval, Antonio Abraços, James Daltrey, and Jen for their comments, questions, and general feedback. We would also like to thank Professor A. A. Long and Professor Chris Gill for their continued mentorship and friendship, the product of which we hope shines through the pages of this book. We also would like to acknowledge the members of the Stoic community who have contributed significantly to our understanding of Stoicism, especially John Sellars, William O. Stephens, and Gregory Lopez.

We will never forget John Butman, our literary agent, who passed away before this book's publication. John took a chance on us when we hadn't yet mastered the art of book-proposal writing. He was as patient as he was steadfast. He was also extremely determined to see this book published because he believed in us and, more importantly, the message we wanted to bring into the world. We can only hope that *Being Better* does his hard work justice. We would also like to thank his son, Jeremy, who helped us in the late stages of the proposal framing. Likewise, we are grateful to our second literary agent, Lucy Cleland, for agreeing to lead us the rest of the way, and to the whole team at Kneerim & Williams, who continued to believe in us, despite the uncertainty of the Covid-19 pandemic. We are also pleased and excited to belong to the New World Library family and to have been supported by our editor, Jason Gardner; our copyeditor, Jeff Campbell; our publicist, Monique Muhlenkamp; proofreader Tanya Fox; as well as Munro Magruder, Kristen Cashman, Joel Prins, Tona Pearce Myers, and Tracy Cunningham.

I would like to offer three additional acknowledgments. One to my grandmother Sheila, who told me to aim high so that, if I fell, I would fall somewhere in the middle. Sheila, if it wasn't for your life and death, I would not have achieved half of what I have. The other two shout-outs are for Dr. Donna Zuckerberg and Dr. Karen Kelsky. Donna, your book *Not All Dead White Men*, and its rallying cry for the contemporary Stoics to stand up and be counted, was the match that lit my fire. You are one of the reasons Leo and I decided to only focus on those who have consciously and consistently partaken in actions we found to be worthy. As Chimamanda Ngozi Adichie reminds us, the stories we tell and how we tell them matter. Lastly, thank you, Karen, for writing *The Professor Is In*. It was the wake-up call I needed to do more with my academic life than earn a PhD. You showed me that if I wanted to make a difference in the world and secure meaningful employment, I would have to dig deeper and work smarter than I ever imagined.

Leonidas would like to thank his family for their continued love, support, and countless dinners. He thanks his friends for years of ruminations about subtle Stoic technicalities over many pints of beer. He is also grateful to the professors in both the philosophy and the international relations departments of Florida International University, who tolerated his love of Stoicism and political philosophy. Finally, he thanks his cat, Schopenhauer, who often reminds him in not-so-subtle ways to take a break because there is more to life than typing away on a keyboard.

Lastly, and from both Leo and me, thanks to all of you who have encouraged and facilitated contemporary Stoicism through academic articles, book publications, conferences, social media groups, and Stoa fellowships. If *Being Better* was your first venture into Stoicism, we want you to know that there are many more Stoics out there who would love to join you on your journey to *eudaimonia*.

NOTES

Chapter 1: The Promise of the "Good Life"

1. Ryan Holiday and Stephen Hanselman, *The Daily Stoic: 366 Meditations on Wisdom, Perseverance, and the Art of Living* (New York: Penguin, 2016).

2. Please see James B. Stockdale, *Courage Under Fire: Testing Epictetus' Doctrines in a Laboratory of Human Behavior* (Stanford, CA: Hoover Institution Press, 1993); and Stephen J. Costello, "A Sketch of the Stoic Influences on Viktor Frankl's Logotherapy," Modern Stoicism, November 28, 2013, https://modernstoicism.com/features-stoicism-logotherapy.

3. Roosevelt carried the definitively Stoic book *Meditations* by Marcus Aurelius throughout his trip to South America, according to the Theodore Roosevelt Center at Dickinson State University; see https://www .theodorerooseveltcenter.org/Research/Digital-Library/Record/Image Viewer?libID=0284909&imageNo=1.

4. Susan Fowler's original blog piece went viral and led to various interviews on how Stoic philosophy supported her when she took Uber executives to task. See Susan Fowler, "Reflecting on One Very Strange Year at Uber" (blog), February 19, 2017, https://www.susanjfowler.com /blog/2017/2/19/reflecting-on-one-very-strange-year-at-uber; and Maureen Dowd, "Susan Fowler: The Uber Whistleblower That Spoke Out about Sexual Harassment in Silicon Valley," *Independent*, November 1, 2017, https://www.independent.co.uk/news/long_reads/uber

-sexual-harassment-silicon-valley-susan-fowler-whistleblower
-experiences-taxi-app-us-a8018016.html.

5. These three maxims are stated by Plato in *Charmides* 165.

6. Robin Hard, trans., *Epictetus: Discourses, Fragments, Handbook* (Oxford, UK: Oxford University Press, 2014).

7. For a typical example of an outrageously superficial understanding of Stoicism, see Nellie Bowles, "Why Is Silicon Valley So Obsessed With the Virtue of Suffering?," *New York Times*, March 26, 2019, https://www.nytimes.com/2019/03/26/style/silicon-valley-stoics.html.

8. In 2018, Leo and I coined the term *Silicon Valley Stoicism* to describe the concentrated and sugar-coated entrepreneurial stripped-down version of Stoicism. See Kai Whiting and Leonidas Konstantakos, "Life-Hack Stoicism: Is It Worth It?," *The Partially Examined Life* (blog), April 17, 2018, https://partiallyexaminedlife.com/2018/04/17/life-hack-stoicism-is-it-worth-it.

9. Margaret Graver and A. A. Long, trans., *Seneca: Letters on Ethics to Lucilius* (Chicago & London: University of Chicago Press, 2015).

10. With special thanks to Gregory Lopez, James Daltrey, and Dirk Mahling for helping us to formulate the Stoic position in this way.

Chapter 2: Virtue as a Way Forward

1. Cynthia King, trans., *Musonius Rufus: Lectures & Sayings* (NP: Create-Space, 2011).

2. For a typical example of Musonius' approach and teaching style, consider this statement by Epictetus (from *Discourses* 3.23.29) on Musonius' teachings (which was actually written by Arrian quoting Epictetus): "Rufus used to say, 'If you are at leisure to praise me, I speak to no purpose.' And indeed, he used to speak in such a manner, that each of us who heard him supposed that some person had accused us to him; he so precisely hit upon what was done by us, and placed the faults of everyone before his eyes." This version is from Thomas Wentworth Higginson, trans., *The Works of Epictetus. Consisting of His Discourses, in Four Books, The Enchiridion, and Fragments. A Translation from the Greek Based on That of Elizabeth Carter* (boston: Little, Brown, and Co., 1865).

3. Christopher Gill, "What Is Stoic Virtue?," in Patrick Ussher, ed., *Stoicism Today: Selected Writings* (London: Stoicism Today Project, 2014).

4. Julia Annas, *Intelligent Virtue* (Oxford, UK: Oxford University Press, 2011), 8–15.

5. That said, Stoics are open to the idea that *Homo sapiens* may not be the only species capable of excellent character. See Kai Whiting, Leonidas

Konstantakos, Greg Sadler, and Christopher Gill, "Were Neanderthals Rational? A Stoic Approach," *Humanities* 7, no. 2 (April 2018): 39.

6. See Origen, *Contra Celsum* 7.53, and the detailed notes in Keith Seddon, *Epictetus' Handbook and the Tablet of Cebes: Guides to Stoic Living* (New York: Routledge, 2006), 1–6.

7. For more about the relationship between Musonius and Epictetus during the time when Epictetus was enslaved, please read *Discourses* 1.9.29–30.

8. Origen writes (*Contra Celsum* 6.2): "Plato can only be seen in the hands of men who seem to be learned, while Epictetus is admired even by common folk, who have an inclination to receive benefit because they perceive the improvement which his words effect in their lives." See Origen, *Contra Celsum*, trans. Henry Chadwick (Cambridge, UK: Cambridge University Press, 1953).

9. For further information, please read Christopher Gill's introductory notes to Hard, *Epictetus*.

10. For more information, please visit the Pat Tillman Foundation, https://pattillmanfoundation.org.

Chapter 3: Know What's in Your Control (and Isn't!)

1. The term *dichotomy of control* is relatively recent and was popularized by philosophy professor William Irvine. See William B. Irvine, *A Guide to the Good Life: The Ancient Art of Stoic Joy* (Oxford, UK: Oxford University Press, 2009).

2. For more information on the intricacies of this stance, we recommend Seddon, *Epictetus' Handbook*, and Margaret Graver, *Stoicism and Emotion* (Chicago: University of Chicago Press, 2008).

3. See Cicero, *De Finibus* 3.22.

4. For the full text, see Public Law no. 106–26, 113 Stat. 50 (May 4, 1999), https://www.govinfo.gov/content/pkg/PLAW-106publ26/pdf/PLAW -106publ26.pdf.

5. For more about Cato's life, we recommend Rob Goodman and Jimmy Soni, *Rome's Last Citizen: The Life and Legacy of Cato, Mortal Enemy of Caesar* (New York: Macmillan, 2012).

6. Pliny the Elder agreed with Cato's judgment in his book *Natural History*, which was written a hundred years later.

7. This is discussed by Lucan in *Pharsalia*. For further details, we recommend Charles Tesoriero, ed., *Lucan* (Oxford, UK: Oxford University Press, 2010), and A. W. Lintott, "Lucan and the History of the Civil War," *Classical Quarterly* 21, no. 2 (1971): 488–505.

8. For more details, see Plutarch's *Life of Cato the Younger*.

Chapter 4: Recognize Luck

1. This is a modified rendition of Epictetus, *Enchiridion* 53, and Seneca, *Moral Letters* 107.11. It is from Donald Robertson, *The Philosophy of Cognitive-Behavioural Therapy (CBT): Stoic Philosophy as Rational and Cognitive Psychotherapy* (New York: Routledge, 2018).

2. This saying is attributed to both Zeno and Chrysippus. It is found in Hippolytus of Rome, *Refutation of All Heresies* 1.21. Similarly, Seneca explains this Stoic concept in the following manner (*On Anger* 3.16): "An animal struggling against the noose tightens it, a bird nervously shaking off the lime, smears it all over its plumage. There is no yoke so tight that it will not hurt the animal less if it pulls with it than if it fights against it." See John M. Cooper, trans., and J. F. Procopé, ed., *Seneca: Moral and Political Essays* (Cambridge, UK: Cambridge University Press, 1995).

3. Alain de Botton, *The Consolations of Philosophy* (New York: Vintage, 2000/2015), 107–9.

4. For an interesting, in-depth description, via Greek sculptures, of the common injuries faced by ancient sportsmen, see D. W. Masterson, "The Ancient Greek Origins of Sports Medicine," *British Journal of Sports Medicine* 10, no. 4 (1976): 196. Also, Plato mentions the "boys with cauliflower ears" in *Gorgias* 515E.

5. Timon of Phlius, for example, is known to have used satire to joke at Cleanthes' expense. See Dee L. Clayman, *Timon of Phlius: Pyrrhonism into Poetry* (berlin: Walter de Gruyter, 2009), 19–20.

6. For more details, see Chris Fisher "The Winds of Fortuna," *Traditional Stoicism* (blog), September 10, 2016, https://www.traditionalstoicism.com/the-winds-of-fortuna.

7. The exact phrase was "Had there been no Chrysippus, there would have been no Stoa." See Diogenes Laertius, *Lives of the Eminent Philosophers*, trans. Pamela Mensch (Oxford, UK: Oxford University Press, 2018), 7.183.

8. Zanardi was particularly dominant in 1998, winning seven of nineteen races and standing on the podium fifteen times during that stretch.

9. Alex Zanardi's injuries were so mind-blowing that his accident and survival became a case study for NASA's research on the limits of human survival.

10. For more on Zanardi's goals prior to and following his accident, see the Repubblica TV interview, "Alex Zanardi interview schools," YouTube, posted September 14, 2014, https://www.youtube.com/watch?v=TmXJujJEY7w.

Chapter 5: No One Is an Island

1. One of the most comprehensive and easily accessible breakdowns of wealth concentration in American dynasties is offered by the Institute of Policy Studies. We recommend Chuck Collins and Josh Hoxie, "Billionaire Bonanza 2018: Inherited Wealth Dynasties of the United States," Institute for Policy Studies, October 2018, https://inequality.org/wp-content/uploads/2018/11/Billionaire-Bonanza-2018-Report-October-2018.pdf.

2. Wealth-X, "Ultra Wealthy Population Analysis: The World Ultra Wealth Report 2019," September 25, 2019, https://www.wealthx.com/report/world-ultra-wealth-report-2019.

3. This point is raised in the introduction of one of the best books on the subject of success: *The Formula: The Universal Laws of Success* (New York: Little, Brown, and Company, 2018) by the Hungarian American, prize-winning physicist Albert-László Barabási.

4. The best descriptions of Panaetius' family origins can be found in Andrew Erskine, *The Hellenistic Stoa: Political Thought and Action*, 2nd ed. (London: Bloomsbury, 2011). Erskine's book rigorously discusses the development of the Stoic philosophical school and its leaders.

5. Seattle Sounders FC is the twenty-ninth-most-attended soccer club in the world, which places it ahead of the international giants AC Milan, Chelsea, Juventus, and Tottenham Hotspur. The average stadium attendance from 2013 to 2018 was 42,797, which puts it behind only Atlanta in the MLS. See "Seattle Sounders Are 29th-Most Attended Club in World," Seattle Sounders, April 16, 2019, https://www.soundersfc.com/post/2019/04/16/seattle-sounders-are-29th-most-attended-club-world.

6. Nick Hanauer lists his more-conspicuous belongings as six homes, three yachts, and a private jet. See Lauren Dake, "He Has Six Homes. Now This 'Self-Loathing Plutocrat' Wants to Help Those with None," *Guardian*, August 17, 2017, https://www.theguardian.com/us-news/2017/aug/17/seattle-homeless-crisis-nick-hanauer-venture-capitalist. His brother, Adrian, is a minority holder of Seattle's new National Hockey League team and one of the largest shareholders of Cambridge United FC in England. See "Adrian Hanauer," Seattle Sounders, accessed November 18, 2020, https://www.soundersfc.com/team/staff/adrian-hanauer.

7. Kate Goldyn, "Nick Hanauer's Address at 2018 Philosophical Graduation Reception," Department of Philosophy, University of Washington, July 16, 2018, https://phil.washington.edu/news/2018/07/16/nick-hanauers-address-2018-philosophy-graduation-reception-video.

8. Robb Mandelbaum, "Nick Hanauer Wants You to Know Everything

You Know about Economics Is Wrong," *Forbes*, January 23, 2018, https://www.forbes.com/sites/robbmandelbaum/2018/01/23/nick-hanauer-wants-you-to-know-everything-you-know-about-economics-is-wrong.

9. Tim Worstall, "Nick Hanauer's Latest Near Insane Economic Plan," *Forbes*, June 30, 2014, https://www.forbes.com/sites/timworstall/2014/06/30/nick-hanauers-latest-near-insane-economic-plan.

10. The Henry Ford, "Ford's Five-Dollar Day," January 3, 2014, https://www.thehenryford.org/explore/blog/fords-five-dollar-day.

11. These job figures are from January 2015 to September 2019. See Federal Reserve Bank of St. Louis, "All Employees: Leisure and Hospitality: Food Services and Drinking Places in Seattle-Tacoma-Bellevue, WA," FRED, last updated September 18, 2020, https://fred.stlouisfed.org/graph/?g=onot.

12. This longitudinal analysis by the National Bureau of Economic Research involved over fourteen thousand workers employed at wages under eleven dollars an hour in early 2015 as well as some twenty-five thousand employed at wages under thirteen dollars an hour at the conclusion of 2015. See Ekaterina Jardim et al., "Minimum Wage Increases and Individual Employment Trajectories," National Bureau of Economic Research Working Paper Series, no. w25182 (October 2018).

13. Daniel Beekman, "Seattle's Minimum-Wage Hikes Didn't Boost Supermarket Prices, New UW Study Finds," *Seattle Times*, February 6, 2019, https://www.seattletimes.com/seattle-news/politics/seattles-minimum-wage-hikes-didnt-boost-supermarket-prices-new-uw-study-says.

14. Ekaterina Jardim and Emma van Inwegen, "Payroll, Revenue, and Labor Demand Effects of the Minimum Wage," Upjohn Institute working paper, no. 19-298 (February 2019).

15. See "Dan Price, Founder & CEO of Gravity Payments," Gravity Payments, accessed November 18, 2020, https://gravitypayments.com/dan-price.

16. Dan Price arrived at this figure based on a Princeton University study. See Daniel Kahneman and Angus Deaton, "High Income Improves Evaluation of Life but Not Emotional Well-Being," *Proceedings of the National Academy of Sciences* 107, no. 38 (2010): 16,489–93.

17. Profits and revenue also increased as did the customer retention rate and general interest in Gravity Payments following the national coverage that sprang out of Dan Price's decision. See Paul Keegan, "Here's What Really Happened at That Company That Set a $70,000 Minimum Wage," *Inc.*, November 2015, https://www.inc.com/magazine/201511/paul-keegan/does-more-pay-mean-more-growth.html.

18. *The Daily Show with Trevor Noah*, season 21, episode 22, aired November 10, 2015, on Comedy Central.

Chapter 6: Put People in Circles, Not Boxes

1. For a list of the qualities that the Stoic teacher Quintus Junius Rusticus cultivated in Marcus Aurelius, see *Meditations* 1.7.

2. Of particular interest to Marcus Aurelius were the words of Epictetus, who is thought to have known his Stoic teacher Rusticus, and those of Aristo of Chios, one of Zeno of Citium's students. See Donald Robertson, *How to Think Like a Roman Emperor: The Stoic Philosophy of Marcus Aurelius* (New York: St. Martin's Press, 2019).

3. This is explained in detail in the list of qualities Marcus tried to nourish and integrate into his own life and character; see *Meditations* book 1.

4. Lucius' ancient biographer states, for instance, that he would "dice the whole night through" and that "he had a golden statue made of the 'Green' horse Volucer, and this he always carried around with him" to show his support for the green chariot team. See *The Life of Lucius Verus*, *Historia Augusta* 4.6 and 6.3, respectively.

5. This quote is from Aulus Gellius, *Attic Nights* ix.5.8. Interestingly, Aulus Gellius was taught by Fronto, the grammarian and rhetoric teacher who also instructed Marcus and Lucius.

6. For a more detailed analysis of this Stoic calling, we recommend A. A. Long, "The Concept of the Cosmopolitan in Greek & Roman Thought," *Daedalus* 137, no. 3 (Summer 2008): 50–58.

7. The Roman physician Galen describes the plague symptoms as fever, diarrhea, and pharyngitis, as well as a skin eruption. Modern scholars generally consider this plague to be smallpox. See R. Flemming, "Galen and the Plague," in *Galen's Treatise Περὶ Ἀλυπίας (De indolentia) in Context*, ed. Caroline Petit (Leiden, The Netherlands: Brill, 2019): 219–44.

8. Although we should read his passages with care and an open mind, Cassius Dio in *Roman History* 72 provides an in-depth description of the various ruckuses that Marcus and his men had to deal with along the Danube.

9. For more on the Germanic tribes, we recommend András Mócsy, *Pannonia and Upper Moesia: A History of the Middle Danube Provinces of the Roman Empire* (New York: Routledge, 1974/2014).

10. Marcus disliked the blood spectacle of sporting combat so much that he requested that gladiators fight with blunt swords so as not to risk their lives in the arena. See Cassius Dio, *Roman History* 72.29. For an in-depth discussion, see M. Carter, "Gladiatorial Combat with 'Sharp' Weapons

($\tau o\hat{\iota}\varsigma$ ὀξέσι σιδήροις)," *Zeitschrift für Papyrologie und Epigraphik* (2006): 161–75. This certainly brings into question any claims that Marcus committed "genocide" against early Christians by sending them to their deaths in the arena. See Donald Robertson, "Did Marcus Aurelius Persecute the Christians?" (blog), January 13, 2017, https://donaldrobertson .name/2017/01/13/did-marcus-aurelius-persecute-the-christians.

11. Lizzie Wade, "Many Imperial Romans Had Roots in the Middle East, Genetic History Shows," *Science*, November 7, 2019, https://www .sciencemag.org/news/2019/11/many-imperial-romans-had-roots -middle-east-genetic-history-shows.

12. When Chobani began operations, the Greek yogurt market constituted half a percent of the total yogurt market. Now it's more than 50 percent.

13. Stephanie Strom, "At Chobani, Now It's Not Just the Yogurt That's Rich," *New York Times*, April 26, 2016, https://www.nytimes.com /2016/04/27/business/a-windfall-for-chobani-employees-stakes-in -the-company.html.

14. Hamdi Ulukaya, "The Anti-CEO Playbook," TED Talk, April 2019, https://www.ted.com/talks/hamdi_ulukaya_the_anti_ceo_playbook.

Chapter 7: Only the Educated Are Free

1. For more on Stoicism as an art of living, we recommend John Sellars, *The Art of Living: The Stoics on the Nature and Function of Philosophy* (London: Bristol Classical Press, 2009).

2. Epictetus, for instance, states in *Discourses* 1.4.13–14: "That's quite enough of you and your weights. What I want to see is what you have achieved by use of those jumping weights. In other words, don't show me your dumbbells. Show me your shoulders!"; Hard, *Epictetus*.

3. The ancient Greek historian Herodotus, in *The Histories* 4.53, waxes lyrically on attributes of the Borysthenes River (now the Dnieper River).

4. One of Sphaerus' definitions is that of "courage" as recorded by Cicero (*Tusculan Disputations* 4.24.53): "Examine the definitions of courage: you will find it does not require the assistance of passion. Courage is, then, an affection of mind that endures all things, being itself in proper subjection to the highest of all laws; or it may be called a firm maintenance of judgment in supporting or repelling everything that has a formidable appearance, or a knowledge of what is formidable or otherwise, and maintaining invariably a stable judgment of all such things, so as to bear them or despise them."

5. One of these Alexandrian debates was recorded by Diogenes Laertius (*Lives of the Eminent Philosophers* 7.177): "When he had made considerable progress in his studies he went to Alexandria, to the court of

Ptolemy Philopator. One day, during a discussion of whether the wise man would hold an opinion, Sphaerus said he would not. The king, who wished to refute him, ordered some waxen pomegranates to be put on the table. Sphaerus was fooled and the king shouted that he had assented to a false impression. To this Sphaerus made a clever reply, saying that what he had assented to was not that they were pomegranates, but that it was reasonable to assume that they were pomegranates, and that there was a difference between the direct apprehension and the probable one"; Laertius, *Lives of the Eminent Philosophers*, trans. Mensch.

6. For this telling of Sphaerus' adventures in Sparta, we are particularly indebted to Plutarch's *Lives of Agis and Kleomenes* and Andrew Erskine, *The Hellenistic Stoa: Political Thought and Action*, 2nd ed. (London: Bloomsbury, 2011), especially chap. 6.

7. For more on Spartan culture, we recommend Anton Powell, ed., *A Companion to Sparta* (hoboken, NJ: John Wiley & Sons, 2018).

8. For more on the role of Stoicism in Spartan education and society, we recommend Nigel M. Kennell, *The Gymnasium of Virtue: Education and Culture in Ancient Sparta* (Chapel Hill: University of North Carolina Press, 1995).

Chapter 8: Live According to Nature

1. I. G. Kidd, ed., *Posidonius, Volume III* (Cambridge, UK: Cambridge University Press, 1999); see fragment 186.

2. This statement is part of Cicero's *Hortensius* (also known as *On Philosophy*), a dialogue that has been lost to history.

3. For more on Pompey's philosophy, we recommend the excellent book by Kit Morrell, *Pompey, Cato, and the Governance of the Roman Empire* (Oxford, UK: Oxford University Press, 2017).

4. For example, see Seneca, *Letters to Lucilius* 87.31–35.

5. Hermann Strasburger writes that Posidonius' aim was "to create not just a beautiful academic theory but a constructive contribution to the solution of the world's political problems"; Hermann Strasburger, "Poseidonios on Problems of the Roman Empire," *Journal of Roman Studies* 55 (November 1965): 40–53.

6. For more on the nuances of pantheistic theism in Stoic physics, we recommend Kai Whiting and Leonidas Konstantakos, "Stoic Theology: Revealing or Redundant?," *Religion* 10, no. 3 (March 2019), and A. A. Long, *Epictetus: A Stoic and Socratic Guide to Life* (Oxford, UK: Clarendon Press, 2002), 147.

7. Frans de Waal, *The Age of Empathy: Nature's Lessons for a Kinder Society* (New York: Random House, 2010), 63.

8. For example, see Cicero, *On the Nature of the Gods*.

9. For an in-depth analysis of Posidonius' contribution to Stoic physics, we recommend Stephen White, "Posidonius and Stoic Physics," *Bulletin of the Institute of Classical Studies*, supplement, no. 94 (2007): 35–76. See also the various works by I. G. Kidd, who has, by far, the most comprehensive analysis on Posidonius' life.

10. For more information on the Cambridge Central Mosque, please visit https://cambridgecentralmosque.org.

11. For a brief depiction of Hazrat Inayat Khan's principles, see "Ten Sufi Thoughts," Inayatiyya, accessed November 18, 2020, https://inayatiorder.org/teachings/ten-sufi-thoughts.

12. Leo and I would like to thank Professor Chris Gill for this insight he shared at Stoicon 2019 in Athens.

13. We encourage you to check out my discussion on the difficulty of buying sustainable items in the following podcast interview: Alex MacLellan, "Interview with Kai Whiting," parts 1–3, episodes 19–21, Stoic Psychology Podcast, February 2020, https://stoicpsychology.buzzsprout.com. In the podcast, we talk about Alex's experience of (not) buying a backpack, which he called "backpack-gate."

14. For more on the psychological benefits of the Swamp Apes initiative, we recommend Manisha Joshi and Joshua Z. Goldman, "Endure, Evolve, Achieve: Stakeholder Perspectives on the Effectiveness of the Swamp Apes Program in Restoring Biopsychosocial Functioning of American Veterans," *Cogent Psychology* 6, no. 1 (2019). See also https://www.swampapes.org.

Chapter 9: Well on the Way to a Life Transformed...

1. Laertius, *Lives of the Eminent Philosophers*, trans. Mensch.

2. Marcus Aurelius, *Meditations*, trans. Robin Hard (Oxford, UK: Oxford University Press, 2011).

3. This quote is from a 1676 letter Newton wrote to Robert Hooke.

4. On the contrary, Diogenes the Cynic believed that as we age we should put more effort into our character. He said: "Give up philosophy because I'm an old man? It's at the end of the race that you break into a burst of speed"; Guy Davenport, *The Guy Davenport Reader* (berkeley, CA: Counterpoint, 2013).

5. For such situations, Epictetus offers very useful advice in *Discourses* 2.8.23–29.

INDEX

acceptance, 45–46

accountability, 6

Achebe, Chinua, 103

action: best, 16–17, 50–51; education and, 107; not taking, 54, 54n; outcomes of, 33–35; problem-solving, 47; right, 51–52; Stoicism in, 58, 102, 107; taking, 5, 54, 54n; virtue as excellence in, 19, 21, 27, 132–33

Adichie, Chimamanda Ngozi, 102–4

adults, role of, 93

Afghanistan War (2001–), 30

Agesistrata (Spartan female leader), 98, 98n, 99, 99n

Agiatis (Agis's wife), 99–100, 102

aging, 127–28, 132–33, 148n4

Agis IV (Spartan king), 97–99, 100, 101, 102

agoge (Spartan educational system), 3, 101

alcohol, 38n

Alexandria (Egypt), 96, 146–47n5

Allah, 115–16

Amazon.com, 67

anarchy, 33n

animals, 113

Annas, Julia, 22

antibribery laws, 39

Antioch (Syria), 86

Antipater of Tarsus, 64

Antonine plague, 85, 145n7

Antonius Pius (Roman emperor), 81, 82, 84

apatheia, 46

apathy, 46

archer analogy, 35–37

Archidamia (Spartan female leader), 97, 98, 98n, 99

arete (excellence), 22

aristocracy, 39n

Aristo of Chios, 145n2

ABOUT THE AUTHORS

Kai Whiting is a lecturer and researcher in Stoicism and sustainability at Université catholique de Louvain in Belgium. To relax, he enjoys building with Lego bricks, watching the kids' program *Lego Ninjago* in multiple languages, and reading Robert Muchamore's Cherub series in Portuguese. His favorite bands are Duran Duran and Soda Stereo, both of which were famous before he was born. If money were no object, he would plant enough trees to tackle climate breakdown, rescue foxes and red pandas, and buy the NFL team the Jacksonville Jaguars.

Leonidas Konstantakos is a lecturer in the Arts and Philosophy department at Miami Dade College. He also conducts research on Stoicism's application to just war theory in the International Relations department at Florida International University. He is proud to have served alongside some of America's best soldiers through two tours of duty in the Iraq War, though he is not proud of the foreign policy that sent them to Iraq in the first place.